Homesteading Harmony

Transform Your Backyard into a Self-Sufficient Haven

Sarah Mitchell

Table of Contents

INTRODUCTION

This is "Homesteading Harmony: Transform Your Backyard into a Self-Sufficient Haven." A rising number of people want to establish a self-sufficient sanctuary in their backyards, embrace sustainability, and reestablish a connection with the earth amid the chaos of modern life. This e-book is your roadmap to a life-changing adventure into the homesteading world, where the natural rhythms blend with everyday rhythms.

"Homesteading Harmony" is more than just conventional gardening and chicken farming. It involves developing a way of life that supports independence, environmental consciousness, and a strong bond with the land. Regardless of the size of your backyard or metropolitan area, this guide will show you how to create, organize, and maintain your self-sufficient retreat.

We'll go over the fundamentals of homesteading in the introductory chapters so you can grasp the spirit of this way of life and how it might affect you. We'll dive into the art of planning, helping you create a workable homestead layout that supports your aspirations for independence.

Essential homesteading abilities will be revealed as we go along, from developing a green thumb to understanding the fundamentals of animal husbandry. We'll walk you through starting your food production, offering advice on creating fruit orchards, vegetable gardens, and innovative gardening techniques that maximize available areas.

However, homesteading is a comprehensive strategy for sustainable living beyond simply sowing seeds and caring for cattle. The art of gathering and conserving your harvest, do-it-yourself projects, and energy and water independence will all be covered in later chapters. We'll look at overcoming obstacles, modifying homesteading methods for urban settings, and creating a welcoming homesteading community.

"Homesteading Harmony" is an invitation to change your way of life, lessen your environmental impact, and strengthen your sense of community rather than just a manual. Come along with us on this enlightening adventure, where we'll walk you through each step and provide you with the inspiration and ideas you need to transform your backyard into a flourishing, self-sufficient oasis. Prepare to welcome the peaceful fusion of homesteading and the natural world into your daily existence.

CHAPTER I

The Foundations of Homesteading

Understanding the Homesteading Lifestyle

Individuals looking for a more fundamental connection to the land, a self-sufficient existence, and an escape from the trappings of modern urban living are likely to find the homesteading lifestyle to be a concept that has stood the test of time. Homesteading originates in the historical setting of pioneers establishing their claims in the American West. It has developed into a conscious and intentional way of life that transcends geographical limits in the modern period. This section delves into the fundamental concepts, reasons, and transforming impact of the homesteading lifestyle on individuals who choose to embrace it. It covers the complexities of the homesteading lifestyle.

In its most fundamental form, homesteading is a holistic way of life that emphasizes self-sufficiency, sustainability, and a harmonious interaction with the natural world. In the modern day, homesteading can occur in various settings, including rural, suburban, and even urban areas, in contrast to isolated cabins on the frontier. The desire to take charge of one's food production, lessen one's reliance on resources from the outside world, and cultivate a more profound connection to the natural world is at the heart of this way of life.

Culturing a plot of land to produce food is one of the fundamental principles underpinning homesteading. By meticulously designing and tending to gardens with fruits, vegetables, and herbs, the homesteader takes on the role of custodian of the earth surrounding their property. The hands-on approach to agriculture not only offers a direct source of sustenance, but it also instills a great respect for the changing of the seasons, the patterns of weather, and the cycles of growth and harvesting.

The practice of homesteading includes not just gardening but also the raising of animals. It is standard practice among homesteaders to raise chickens for eggs, goats for milk, or even larger livestock for meat. This is done for a variety of reasons. Individuals are allowed to become acquainted with the responsibilities of caring for live creatures through this lifestyle component, which helps to cultivate a sense of connection to the animals that contribute to the nutrition of the homestead.

Numerous factors contribute to the decision to adopt a lifestyle characterized by homesteading. Pursuing more autonomy and independence is a common motivation for many people. The ability of homesteaders to lessen their dependency on external supply chains and mitigate the impact of external economic forces on their day-to-day lives is achieved through the cultivation of their food and the generation of resources on their sites. This level of self-sufficiency not only gives one a feeling of safety but also fits with the aspiration to lead a more purposeful and deliberate life.

In addition to achieving self-sufficiency, homesteading frequently demonstrates a dedication to environmentally responsible ways of living. Homesteaders consciously decide to reduce their ecological footprint in this day and age, characterized by ongoing concerns about the environment and climate change. They integrate their lifestyle choices with a more significant commitment to environmental care by adopting regenerative agricultural techniques, implementing water conservation measures, and exploring alternative energy sources.

At the same time, the homesteading way of life represents a revival of old methods of production and craftsmanship. There is a revival of practical knowledge among individuals as they take on roles such as gardeners, carpenters, and animal caregivers. Having a renaissance of hands-on skills helps individuals become more self-sufficient and also helps individuals develop a profound sense of empowerment and accomplishment.

Beyond the apparent dimensions of food production and resource management, the homesteading lifestyle has a transforming impact that extends beyond those aspects. A greater sense of well-being, mental clarity, and a closer connection to the natural world are many of the benefits that homesteaders frequently report experiencing. Research has shown that a reduction in stress levels and an overall increase in mental health can be achieved by engaging in everyday activities that are in sync with the natural cycles of the seasons and the natural rhythms of nature.

In addition, the homesteading way of life helps cultivate a feeling of community and values shared by all. Homesteaders frequently develop networks with other people who share their values and interests, participating in seed exchanges, skill-sharing gatherings, and community-based initiatives to support one another. Homesteaders worldwide are connected through online platforms and social media, creating a virtual village where they may share their experiences, struggles, and victories. This feeling of community transcends geographical limits.

Homesteading has numerous benefits; moreover, it has its share of difficulties. Particularly for individuals not experienced with agriculture, animal husbandry, and sustainable living techniques, the initial learning curve is high. A lifestyle involving the demands of daily chores, the unpredictability of weather, and the duties of caring for animals requires devotion, resilience, and a willingness to embrace the inevitable setbacks inherent in such a lifestyle.

Additionally, homesteading life frequently calls for a fundamental transformation in one's mentality. It is possible to make a considerable divergence from the standards of current society by adopting a lifestyle characterized by simplicity, austerity, and an intentional rejection of consumer-driven culture. The fact of the matter is, however, that this transformation enables individuals to reevaluate their priorities, redefine success, and discover fulfillment in the straightforwardness of a life connected to the land.

In conclusion, homesteading is making a conscious decision to reclaim control over one's life, emphasizing sustainability, and forging a fundamental relationship with the natural world. Homesteading is a philosophy that resonates with those seeking a more meaningful and intentional way of life. It is not only related to the practical issues of food production and resource management but also other aspects. There is a transforming journey that transcends the bounds of time and place that may be experienced via the homesteading lifestyle, regardless of whether it is practiced in expansive rural landscapes or intimate urban quarters. This demonstrates the everlasting human yearning for self-sufficiency, a healthy relationship with the natural world, and a life with purpose and authenticity.

Assessing Your Backyard's Potential

The path to being a homesteader starts at the door of one's backyard, a blank canvas ready to be turned into a self-sufficient refuge. Evaluating your backyard's potential is an essential first step toward peace with homesteading. During this procedure, the available space, the surrounding environment, and your homestead's unique qualities are carefully examined to determine how best to organize and build your homestead. This post aims to provide a healthy balance between nature and sustainable living by reviewing the critical factors and methods to consider when assessing your garden's potential.

Spend some time getting to know the terrain before starting your homesteading journey. Examine your backyard thoroughly, taking note of the geography, the makeup of the soil, and any current features like trees, hills, or water sources. These factors are essential in assessing your area's suitability for specific homesteading pursuits. The kinds of crops you can plant and the sites that work best for buildings, like garden beds or chicken coops, are determined by several criteria, including well-drained soil, plenty of sunlight, and shielding from strong winds.

Taking Sunlight and Microclimates into Account A healthy homestead depends heavily on sunlight, which affects everything from plant development to an area's suitability for a given activity. Take note of how the light travels through your backyard during the day and as the seasons change. Determine which places are always in the shade, partially shaded, or receive full sun. This evaluation helps with thoughtful garden bed placement, guaranteeing crops that thrive in the sun get the best possible light exposure. Furthermore, pay attention to the microclimates in your backyard—areas where humidity and temperature fluctuate. Comprehending these subtleties enables you to customize your homesteading endeavors to the specific circumstances of your area.

Evaluating Garden Space for Layouts A flourishing vegetable garden is the focal point of many homesteads, and the design of this area is essential to its success. Analyze the space available for possible garden designs, considering elements like closeness to the kitchen, ease of upkeep daily, and weather protection. Companion planting, raised beds, and square-foot gardening are popular methods that maximize available space and increase productivity. Plan your garden layout considering any existing features, such as mature trees or structures that may affect the amount of sunshine that reaches your space.

Setting Up Your Yard for Livestock Zoning becomes essential for individuals who want to live a more complete homesteading lifestyle with cattle. Choose locations that will work for building barns, pens, or coops, and ensure they don't conflict with local zoning laws. Examine the viability of designating specific areas for various animal species, considering aspects like noise pollution, proper disposal of waste, and the requirement for sufficient room for the animals to go around. Creating a harmonious and productive homesteading environment in your backyard requires the seamless integration of these zones.

Rainwater Harvesting and Water Management A productive homestead requires efficient water management. Examine the water sources in your backyard, including hose systems, conventional irrigation, and organic elements like ponds. Examine the viability of rainwater collection, an eco-friendly method that lessens dependency on outside water sources. Analyze the drainage patterns to avoid areas being too wet and ensure that crops and livestock get the right amount of moisture. In addition to protecting the well- being of your homestead, an effective water management plan helps maintain the sustainability of the environment as a whole.

Examining Microclimates and Wind Patterns In homesteading, the wind can be both a friend and an enemy. Examine the predominant wind patterns in your backyard to find any potentially windy spots that can affect the welfare of your animals or the health of your plants. Strategically plant windbreaks utilizing fences, towering plants, or buildings to protect vulnerable locations. Additionally, consider using wind patterns to create microclimates in your garden. You can designate sheltered spaces for delicate plants, young trees, or comfortable places to sit, improving your homestead's general usability and comfort.

Testing and Improving the Soil The soil's health and fertility determine a homestead's success. Do a soil test to assess nutrient levels, pH balance, and potential inadequacies. This analysis helps you select crops that will flourish in your particular soil type and enable you to apply targeted soil amendments. Enhancing soil via composting, cover crops, and organic fertilizers is a great way to support regenerative and sustainable farming practices. The aim is to cultivate soil that supports a wide variety of plants, improves water retention, and supports the health of the ecosystem as a whole.

Taking Safety and Legal Aspects into Account Homesteading is a practice that involves following safety guidelines and local laws in addition to being an artistic endeavor. To ensure you comply, check your local zoning laws and restrictions regarding backyard farming. Certain regions may impose limitations on the kinds of animals that can be kept there, building buildings, or applying specific agricultural techniques. It is best to be aware of these legal factors early to avoid issues later. Furthermore, evaluate safety aspects like the distance from nearby properties to ensure your homesteading endeavors don't endanger or disturb others.

Accepting Biodiversity and Integrating Ecosystems A distinguishing feature of ecological homesteading is the incorporation of biodiversity into the backyard environment. Determine whether your backyard can sustain various plants, helpful insects, and wildlife. To help encourage healthy crop growth and naturally ward off pests, think about companion planting. Establish habitats for pollinators, such as butterflies and bees, to increase your homestead's overall resilience. In addition to enhancing the aesthetic appeal of your garden, biodiversity also helps maintain a healthy ecology, resulting in a harmonic combination of natural beauty and productivity.

To sum up, evaluating your backyard's suitability for homesteading involves a complex procedure that blends strategic preparation with hands-on observation. Every aspect, from zoning for cattle to knowing the topography to managing water resources to the creation of an independent sanctuary, matters. A successful homestead is built on thoroughly assessing soil characteristics, wind patterns, and sunlight. Moreover, you develop a comprehensive and long-lasting approach to homesteading by embracing safety precautions, legal compliance, and biodiversity preservation. When you embark on this transformation journey, evaluating your backyard becomes more than just a practical need. Instead, it becomes an artistic and imaginative undertaking that will shape the landscape on which your harmonious homesteading will take shape.

Setting Goals for Self-Sufficiency

Individuals are motivated to retake control over their means of subsistence, resources, and way of life when they have a strong desire to become self-sufficient, which is at the core of the homesteading lifestyle. Not only is the process of moving to a self-sufficient farm a practical activity, but it is also a journey that is highly intentional and transforming. This section aims to investigate the art of defining goals for self-sufficiency in the context of homesteading. Specifically, we will explore the motives, techniques, and concerns that build a blueprint for achieving harmony between human life and the land.

Self-sufficiency is typically motivated by a desire to break free from the restraints of external dependents and the uncertainties of the modern world. This desire is often the driving force behind the pursuit of financial independence. An increase in the number of people interested in self-sufficiency can be attributed to the realization that there are weaknesses in the food supply chain, economic swings, and environmental concerns. Homesteaders set out on this path to cultivate a way of life based on the ideals of sustainability and resilience, producing their food, generating renewable resources, and developing their energy.

Understanding one's values and motives is the initial stage of establishing objectives for achieving self-sufficiency. The journey of every homesteader is different since personal convictions, worries about the environment, and preferences for lifestyle influence it. Some prioritize food security to produce a significant percentage of their daily nourishment. Some people may concentrate on minimizing their environmental impact, including using renewable energy sources and engaging in agricultural practices that promote regenerative agriculture. To create the groundwork for SMART objectives—specific, measurable, attainable, relevant, and time-bound goals—homesteaders must first define their reasons. These goals should be tailored to the homesteader's vision of self-sufficiency.

When it comes to homesteading, the production of food is an essential component of self-sufficiency. Establishing objectives concerning cultivating fruits, vegetables, and herbs is congruent with establishing a flourishing and sustainable farm. These objectives include the creation of a varied garden layout, optimizing space via raised beds or vertical gardening, and implementing strategies for companion planting to increase productivity. The cultivation of a practical roadmap toward the fulfillment of nutritional demands and the reduction of reliance on external food sources can be accomplished by setting specific targets for the variety and amount of crops for cultivation.

The breeding of cattle is frequently included among the objectives of self-sufficiency, in addition to food production. When it comes to homesteading, some people aim to keep hens for eggs, goats for milk, or even larger cattle for meat. Setting goals for animal husbandry requires considering various factors, including the construction of appropriate shelters, the provision of adequate nutrition, and the management of breeding cycles. These aims contribute to the formation of a symbiotic relationship between the homesteader and their animals and contribute to the diversification and sustainability of the food source.

Because water is a limited and indispensable resource, achieving water self-sufficiency is vital to homesteading objectives. It is consistent with the principles of sustainability to establish goals for collecting rainwater, installing efficient irrigation systems, and implementing water conservation methods. Homesteaders may investigate the possibility of installing rain barrels, porous surfaces, and greywater irrigation systems to lessen the runoff on their property. Homesteaders can improve the resilience of their operations by focusing on water self-sufficiency. This is especially important in places prone to water scarcity or supply changes.

Independence from energy sources is another aspect of self-sufficiency that homesteaders frequently place a high priority on. Setting goals for renewable energy sources, such as solar panels or wind turbines, is one way to contribute to a more sustainable and environmentally beneficial homestead. These objectives will likely involve determining the amount of energy required, developing systems that use natural resources, and progressively shifting toward a reduced reliance on the power generated by the grid. Not only does energy self-sufficiency correlate with environmental conscience, but it also reduces the influence that variations in external energy have on the homestead.

Homesteaders usually incorporate tactics for reducing waste and recycling resources into their aims to fulfill their goal of becoming self-sufficient. To reduce the amount of damage done to the environment, it is important to establish goals for composting, recycling, and reusing items. The establishment of effective composting systems, the reuse of materials for construction projects, and the reduction of single-use plastics could be among the goals. Homesteaders contribute to the circular economy of their homestead by recognizing the need for waste minimization. This allows them to utilize resources in a manner that is both sustainable and regenerative.

Establishing objectives for self-sufficiency encompasses the material factors of acquiring food, water, and energy and the acquisition of necessary skills. Knowledge in fields such as permaculture, organic gardening, animal husbandry, and basic carpentry is frequently sought out by homesteaders as they strive to improve their lifestyle. These educational objectives improve the homesteader's capacity to adjust to shifting conditions, find solutions to problems, and continue to live a resilient and self-sufficient life. A sense of continuity and empowerment can be fostered via the pursuit of skills, which aligns with the ageless tradition of handing down practical knowledge from one generation to the next.

The pursuit of self-sufficiency is a worthy activity. Yet, it is vital to balance aspirations and realistic evaluation of resources and constraints to succeed in this quest. The progressive nature of homesteading development is acknowledged by setting attainable goals, which is especially important for individuals who are new to the lifestyle. A sense of progress and success can be achieved by developing gradual milestones, which also helps reduce feelings of exhaustion and overload. Homesteaders need to tailor their goals to the amount of time and money they have available and the specific characteristics of the property they operate on.

Community integration is an essential component when it comes to homesteading and achieving self-sufficiency goals. Even though the vision frequently involves lessening reliance on external systems, establishing a supportive homesteading community adds to the development of resilience and the exchange of information. Homesteaders can establish objectives such as their participation in neighborhood farmer's markets, their organization of community seminars, or their participation in collaborative endeavors with adjacent homesteads. Pursuing these objectives helps cultivate a sense of connection within the larger community by facilitating the sharing of ideas, resources, and support among its members.

When homesteaders make progress on their path toward self-sufficiency, they need to reevaluate their intentions and make adjustments to their goals periodically. Variations in the climate, shifts in the economy, or personal circumstances are examples of external factors that may impact the level of achieveability of particular objectives. Adaptability and flexibility are two of the most essential elements in homesteading because they enable individuals to readjust their goals in response to changing circumstances. To achieve long-term success and fulfillment as a self-sufficient homesteader, it is essential to possess the ability to learn from experiences, accept challenges, and alter goals by changing circumstances.

Setting goals for self-sufficiency in homesteading is a subtle and dynamic process that connects personal beliefs, motivations, and lifestyle choices with tangible and measurable objectives. In conclusion, this includes establishing goals that are attainable and measurable. Each objective contributes to the broader vision of a harmonious and self-sufficient homestead. These objectives range from the production of food and the management of water to the independence from energy and the elimination of waste. The conscious development of skills, incorporating community assistance, and acknowledging realistic limitations are all essential components in developing a blueprint for homesteading harmony. The goal-setting process becomes not only a practical blueprint for homesteaders as they navigate this transforming path, but it also becomes a conscious and intentional expression of commitment to a more sustainable, resilient, and self-sufficient way of life.

CHAPTER II

Planning Your Homestead

Designing a Functional Homestead Layout

Creating a practical homestead plan is like building a sustainable, efficient, and environmentally friendly symphony. When people become homesteaders, they face the challenge of turning their backyard into a self-sufficient sanctuary. The plan serves as a canvas on which the homesteader paints a picture of a landscape that harmoniously and thoughtfully combines living areas, livestock pastures, gardens, and water features. In this section, we delve into the strategic choices that mold the outward expression of self-sufficiency as we examine the ideas and factors that guide creating a workable homestead plan.

Careful design and zone identification are the cornerstones of a well-functioning homestead layout. Proximity to the home is a crucial factor to consider, as it impacts everyday management and accessibility. Setting aside areas for particular uses, such as social areas, gardening, and animal husbandry, makes dividing the farm into manageable, functional sections easier. Homesteaders must consider elements like wind patterns, sunshine exposure, and the water's natural flow through the landscape when planning their layout.

The location and arrangement of the vegetable garden are essential aspects of the farmhouse layout. The foundation of self-sufficiency is the garden, which offers a ready supply of fresh produce. Homesteaders need to measure the area they have for gardening, considering elements like sunlight, the condition of the soil, and ease of access. Designing a garden with companion planting and crop rotation techniques can maximize output and naturally reduce pests. Raised beds and container gardening are other options for making space most available and minimizing maintenance.

A thorough homestead design must include livestock areas, especially for individuals who hope to raise animals for food, fiber, or company. When creating functional places for cattle, factors like sufficient shelter, grounds for grazing, and effective waste management must be considered. The strategic location of barns, paddocks, and chicken coops should consider wind patterns, accessibility for cleaning and feeding, and the animals' integration into the larger environment. Well-planned livestock zones improve the homestead's general functionality as well as the welfare of the animals.

Water management, which includes resource saving and thoughtful feature placement, is crucial in homestead layout design. Water can be captured and directed for irrigation using ponds, swales, or rainwater collection devices. Waterlogging and erosion can be avoided by designing the land to accommodate the water's natural flow. It is possible to incorporate water-efficient irrigation methods, like soaker hoses or drip irrigation, into the design to reduce water waste and promote the well-being of cattle and crops.

The homestead layout's communal areas are essential for creating community and relaxation. These areas, which can include a fire pit for socializing, a contemplative garden for quiet times, or a unique dining spot for the family, all improve the general well-being of the homesteader and their neighborhood. Shade, wind protection, and incorporating visually appealing aspects that enhance the homestead's visual appeal should all be considered during the design process. The hub of the homestead is its communal areas, which promote interaction and deepen the ties that bind those who live and work there.

Many areas of homestead layout design are influenced by the permaculture philosophy, which emphasizes building regenerative and sustainable ecosystems. Designing with knowledge of the land's natural patterns and resources is crucial to integrating permaculture concepts. This could involve planning areas that resemble natural ecosystems, growing perennial crops, and developing polyculture gardens. The goals of permaculture design are to reduce waste, increase efficiency, and strengthen the ecosystem's overall resilience on the farm.

Microclimates have an impact on agricultural success and animal welfare. Hence, they must be taken into account when designing a homestead layout. Microclimates are specific climatic conditions impacted by surrounding structures, flora, and topography. Homesteaders can strategically plant delicate plants, protect animals from inclement weather, and create cozy outdoor areas by designing with microclimates in mind. The homestead plan becomes a dynamic, responsive system that adjusts to the subtleties of the surroundings by utilizing the advantages of microclimates.

Pathways and accessibility are essential but frequently disregarded aspects of designing a homestead layout. The homestead's various zones are connected by well-planned walkways, which make movement more accessible and reduce soil compaction in high-traffic areas. The layout should consider the usage of wheelbarrows, tools, and other equipment, ensuring that the walkways are sufficiently broad and kept up. Accessibility improves the effectiveness of daily tasks and adds to the homestead's overall usefulness.

Security and fences are essential when designing a homestead layout, especially if you are raising cattle. Carefully constructed fencing establishes boundaries, protects animals from predators, and improves the homestead's general security. The layout should consider the various requirements of the many animals, including elements like electric fencing, predator-proof enclosures, or organic obstacles. The homesteader's peace of mind and the health of the flora and fauna are enhanced by security measures.

Seasonality is a significant factor in homestead layout design; it affects choices about planting dates, shade structures, and where to put seasonal crops. By considering seasonal variations in their designs, homesteaders may maximize the land's productivity all year round. This could entail crop rotation by seasonal growth patterns, preparing for wind protection during the colder months, and placing deciduous trees strategically to provide shade in the summer and sunlight in the winter. The homestead layout is kept dynamic and sensitive to the ever-changing cycles of nature by considering seasonal factors.

A fundamental idea in homestead plan design is adaptability, which recognizes that the terrain will change with time. The original design should incorporate flexibility for growth, experimentation, and modifications in response to the homesteader's changing requirements and experiences.

Homesteaders may decide to change the design as they get knowledge and experience to make room for additional buildings, cattle, or crops. A thoughtfully planned homestead layout encourages flexibility, enabling ongoing enhancement and the integration of acquired knowledge.

In summary, creating a functioning homestead layout entails combining various components thoughtfully and deliberately to produce a peaceful, self-sufficient setting. Every choice about the location of gardens and livestock areas, water management, communal areas, and microclimates adds to the homestead's overall resilience and functionality. Understanding the land's natural patterns should be the foundation of the design, with an emphasis on adaptability and permaculture principles. Homesteaders create a living canvas that embodies their beliefs, goals, and dedication to a self-sufficient and peaceful way of life as they begin the design process.

Selecting Suitable Crops and Livestock

The choice of cattle and crops in the complex fabric of homesteading is fundamental to sustainability, self-sufficiency, and a peaceful coexistence with the land. Homesteaders set out on a cultivation voyage, carefully selecting which flora and fauna will flourish in their particular setting and add to the ecosystem's overall resilience. This section explores the symbiotic link between the homesteader, the land, and the biological species that inhabit it. It does this by delving into the ideas and factors that influence the selection of suitable crops and cattle.

A self-sufficient farmhouse is built on crops, which offer diversity, nutrition, and a direct link to the natural cycles. Choosing appropriate crops requires careful evaluation of the available growing season, soil composition, and climate. While crops like potatoes, carrots, and cruciferous vegetables may do better in colder areas, staples like tomatoes, peppers, and leafy greens may thrive in temperate climates. Homesteaders should also think about the nutritional content of their crops, trying to grow a variety that will suit their family's needs.

Many homesteaders choose their crops based on the principles of permaculture, which emphasize the development of regenerative and sustainable ecosystems. The development of perennial crops is encouraged by permaculture principles since they demand less annual input and improve the soil's general health. A resilient homestead must have fruit trees, berry bushes, and perennial herbs since they increase biodiversity and produce long-term yields. Crop choice is in line with the tenets of regenerative agriculture, which support the preservation of water, the health of the soil, and the advancement of natural cycles.

When establishing a farm, crop rotation is a strategic factor that helps to maintain healthy soil and keep pests and diseases from growing. Homesteaders reduce the danger of soil erosion and increase the land's overall production by rotating their crops on a seasonal basis.

Peas and beans are examples of legumes that help the soil fix nitrogen, which benefits later crops. Root crops, such as carrots and radishes, improve the structure of compacted soil by breaking it up. Crop rotation is carefully planned to provide a sustainable and equitable utilization of the homestead's growing areas.

The companion planting technique, which emphasizes the symbiotic interactions between several plant species, is rooted in conventional agricultural knowledge. Homesteaders can increase overall yield, boost nutrient uptake, and strengthen pest resistance by carefully matching crops that complement one another. For instance, putting beans next to corn provides natural nitrogen fixation, while planting fragrant herbs like basil beside tomatoes might discourage pests. Companion plant choosing becomes a subtle art form that improves the homestead garden's harmony and health.

Herbs and medicinal plants are frequently included in homesteaders' gardens, together with annual and perennial crops. Herbs are helpful for cooking but have therapeutic and fragrant properties. The homesteader's cooking is enhanced by choices like lavender, chamomile, and mint, which also serve as natural treatments and improve the homestead's whole sensory experience. Herb farming incorporates the therapeutic qualities of plants into daily life, adhering to the ideals of holistic living.

Another essential component of homesteading is choosing appropriate livestock, which broadens the ecology of the homestead to include creatures that support soil fertility, food production, and a healthy ecological cycle. The livestock selection is influenced by several variables, including the homesteader's tastes and skill level, the environment, local laws, and available space. Chickens are a popular choice for eggs and meat because of their adaptability and low maintenance requirements. In addition to producing milk, goats' grazing practices help manage the soil and control weeds. Mature animals, like pigs or cows, provide milk, meat, and more chances to enhance the soil through rotational grazing.

Taking care of animals requires a dedication to their welfare and moral treatment. Access to clean water, sufficient diet, and adequate shelter are essential when choosing and caring for animals. Livestock on a homestead is successful and sustainable because of the homesteader's knowledge of animal behavior, health monitoring, and provision of suitable living circumstances. Humans and animals develop a mutually beneficial connection in which each party gains from the contributions and services of the other.

To further their self-sufficiency objectives, homesteaders frequently consider smaller, unconventional animals in addition to regular cattle. For instance, rabbits provide a sustainable source of meat and fur, and their dung may be used to fertilize gardens. Bees improve the general health of the homestead garden by aiding in pollination and honey production. Including various animal species in the homestead ecosystem adds resilience and complexity consistent with permaculture and biodiversity concepts.

Holistic land management and rotational grazing principles guide livestock integration into the larger homestead ecology. Rotational grazing allows pastures to regenerate and improves the general health of the soil by transferring animals over different areas of the land. Homesteaders maximize resource utilization, avoid overgrazing, and aid soil regeneration by imitating natural grazing patterns. The deliberate integration of livestock into the landscape promotes a harmonious coexistence of animals and the environment, which becomes a dynamic and regenerative practice.

Humane and moral methods of caring for animals are part of the consideration for animal welfare, which goes beyond their fundamental needs. Livestock are more likely to be healthy overall when they have access to open spaces, acceptable living circumstances, and less needless stress. To guarantee that the animals have happy and healthy lives, homesteaders frequently implement techniques like mobile coops, rotating paddocks, and humane means of killing. The ethical aspects of livestock management reflect the homesteader's dedication to the honest and caring care of all living things.

The selection of animals also supports the homesteader's overarching objectives of sustainability and resource efficiency. Through their grazing practices, livestock—especially ruminants like goats and sheep—can aid in managing the land. Homesteaders utilize the innate tendencies of livestock to preserve a healthy environment by dividing and allocating their animals across various areas of the land in a deliberate manner. Manure Animals become priceless resources for crop fertilization, completing the nutrient cycle and lowering the need for outside inputs.

Animal waste products are used in closed-loop systems like aquaponics and vermiculture to promote plant growth, demonstrating how animals may coexist peacefully on a homestead. Vermicomposting is the process by which worms convert organic materials into nutrient-rich castings suitable for fertilizer use. Aquaponics systems integrate hydroponic plant cultivation with fish farming, whereby plant waste supplies nutrients to the fish, and the plants purify fish water. These integrated systems embody the interdependent ties seen in a sustainable homestead, where waste from one component becomes an essential resource for another.

Since different components of the environment are interdependent, homesteaders sometimes aim for a diverse and integrated strategy for raising cattle and crops. Combining trees and shrubs with crops and cattle is known as agroforestry, and it's becoming a comprehensive method for increasing sustainability and productivity. In addition to being a reliable source of food, fruit and nut trees enhance the homestead's overall biodiversity. A homesteader's dedication to establishing a robust and well-balanced ecosystem is demonstrated by the thoughtful selection and arrangement of crops and livestock in the setting of agroforestry.

In summary, choosing appropriate livestock and crops is a complex and intertwined part of homesteading, where the homesteader takes on the role of custodian of the land and its living occupants. The concepts of permaculture, agroecology, and ethical animal husbandry guide the decisions to establish a peaceful and fruitful homestead ecosystem. The decisions made by homesteaders demonstrate a dedication to sustainable, regenerative, and self-sufficient living. These decisions range from the thoughtful selection of crops that flourish in particular climates to incorporating a variety of livestock species that support soil fertility and ecological balance. The homesteader learns to maintain a healthy and balanced environment and be a land cultivator through this complex dance with nature.

Considering Sustainable Practices

The sustainability ethos, a guiding concept in the field, shapes the homesteader's path. The dedication to sustainable living demonstrates a profound awareness of the interdependence between human pursuits and environmental health, from resource management to agricultural techniques. This section discusses the value of considering sustainable practices when homesteading and looks at how these methods affect a self-sufficient homestead's long-term viability, production, and resilience.

A deep regard for the land and its natural processes is essential to sustainable homesteading. As a living, dynamic ecosystem, soil health is prioritized in sustainable farming practices. Using organic and regenerative techniques instead of synthetic pesticides and fertilizers promotes soil fertility, microbial diversity, and the general balance of ecosystems. Composting, crop rotation, and cover crops improve soil structure, water retention, and nutrient cycling and are, therefore, essential elements of sustainable agriculture. Homesteaders support the larger objective of environmental stewardship and ensure their land's production by promoting the soil's health.

Sustainable homesteading places a high value on water conservation, especially when water supplies are erratic or scarce. Techniques like mulching, drip irrigation, and rainwater collection reduce water waste and encourage effective use of this valuable resource. Rainfall harvesting systems lessen dependency on outside water sources by collecting and storing rainfall for later use in irrigation. Drip irrigation reduces evaporation and maximizes moisture absorption by directing water straight to the roots of plants. By applying organic materials to the soil's surface, a process known as mulching, soil erosion can be avoided, and water absorption can be improved. In addition to maintaining the homestead's health, these sustainable water methods support appropriate water stewardship.

Sustainable homesteading is centered on energy efficiency and renewable energy sources, which align with the overarching objective of lowering dependency on non-renewable resources. Homesteaders frequently incorporate solar panels, wind turbines, or other alternative energy sources to address their power needs. A smaller ecological footprint is achieved by using energy-efficient appliances, off-grid system installation, and the design of energy-efficient buildings. A self-sufficient lifestyle is supported by incorporating renewable energy sources, which also lessen the impact of energy fluctuations on the homestead. Using these techniques, sustainable homesteading proves the viability of eco-friendly living and is an example of responsible energy use.

Essential components of sustainable homesteading are waste reduction and recycling, which demonstrate a dedication to reducing environmental effects and developing closed-loop systems. Composting turns yard trash and kitchen scraps into beneficial soil additions by breaking down organic waste into nutrient-rich compost. Composting improves soil fertility and lessens the demand for external fertilizers in gardening. Reusing products for different purposes, recycling building materials, and reducing single-use plastic usage all help reduce waste overall. Embracing a zero-waste mentality encourages resource conservation and thoughtful consumption, consistent with sustainable practices.

Recognizing the intrinsic need for varied habitats for ecological balance and resilience, biodiversity becomes a cornerstone of sustainable homesteading. A biodiverse homestead incorporates the planting of a range of crops, the incorporation of fruit and nut trees, and the protection of natural habitats. A balanced environment that reduces the danger of pests and diseases is created by diverse plantings that provide food for birds, insects, and other creatures. Polyculture, the use of native plants, and companion planting all increase biodiversity and promote resilient, flourishing environments. Sustainable homesteading strongly emphasizes biodiversity, which helps safeguard native species and preserve local ecosystems outside of the homestead.

Sustainable homesteading is guided by regenerative agriculture concepts, which emphasize methods that actively improve and restore the health of the land. The homesteading toolset includes rotational grazing, agroforestry, and regenerative soil management. By grazing animals in various areas of the land, rotational grazing helps pastures recover and improves the general health of the soil. Agroforestry creates a comprehensive system that optimizes productivity and sustainability by combining trees, shrubs, crops, and livestock. Building soil organic matter, increasing nutrient cycling, and retaining more water are the main goals of regenerative soil management techniques. Through the implementation of regenerative agricultural practices, homesteaders take an active role in revitalizing and repairing the land they manage.

In sustainable homesteading, self-sufficiency encompasses the on-site production of food, medicine, and other necessities. In addition to meeting the homesteader's nutritional and health needs, growing a wide variety of fruits, vegetables, herbs, and medicinal plants helps to build a resilient and self-sufficient homestead. The homestead pharmacy incorporates herbs and medicinal plants to offer natural cures for common illnesses. The ideas of food sovereignty are aligned with the growth of food-producing plants, which gives the homesteader more control over their food supplies and less reliance on outside systems. Sustainable homesteading reduces the ecological effect of daily living and creates a model for localized resilience by promoting self-sufficiency.

Sustainable homesteading relies heavily on education and community involvement to create a shared knowledge, awareness, and empowering culture. Homesteaders frequently interact with the communities in which they live by offering workshops, exchanging ideas, and working together on projects. Knowledge sharing among homesteaders enhances their ability to adapt and be resilient. A sense of interconnectedness between people and the larger ecosystem is fostered, and environmentally conscious habits are adopted by others as a result of sustainable homesteading acting as a beacon of knowledge.

Sustainable homesteading is guided by holistic land management techniques, emphasizing integrating diverse components into a coherent and regenerative system. Permaculture principles promote the building of regenerative and sustainable ecosystems, which offer a framework for planning homesteads that resemble natural cycles. The homestead ecosystem's general resilience and health are enhanced by its inhabitants' thoughtful selection and arrangement, including plants, animals, and buildings. Homesteaders ensure their methods actively promote the land's regeneration and long-term health by taking a holistic approach.

A fundamental component of sustainable homesteading is the humane treatment of animals, which demonstrates a dedication to caring and conscientious stewardship. In animal husbandry, humane slaughter techniques include giving animals suitable living quarters and access to open areas. Homesteaders prioritize the welfare of their livestock, and they frequently implement techniques like rotating paddocks and mobile coops to ensure the animals have happy, healthy lives. A symbiotic relationship develops when animals are integrated into the homestead ecology, benefiting humans and animals from each other's contributions and services.

CHAPTER III

Essential Homesteading Skills

Cultivating a Green Thumb: Gardening Basics

The art of gardening is more than just sowing seeds; it's a deep connection to the natural world's cycles, a dance between the elements that form life. Being a green thumb involves more than just stirring soil and caring for plants; it also entails comprehending the intricate interactions between sunshine, water, soil, and the many other living things that make up a healthy garden. In this section, we will explore the foundations of gardening, enabling readers to cultivate a relationship with nature, nurture and coax life from the soil, and enjoy the abundant benefits of a well-kept garden.

Understanding soil, the base of all plant life is

fundamental to gardening. Rich in organic matter, air, minerals, and microscopic life, healthy soil is a dynamic ecosystem. The soil's drainage, water-holding capacity, and nutritional content are determined by its composition, broadly classified as sandy, loamy, or clayey. It is essential to evaluate the composition and structure of the soil before planting to ascertain its fertility and plant growth potential. Compost or well-rotted manure are examples of organic matter that can be added to the soil to strengthen its structure, retain more water, and supply vital nutrients for plant growth. For the seeds and seedlings that will bring life to the garden, soil acts as a loving womb.

Gardening depends heavily on sunlight, the radiant

energy that powers all life on Earth. Understanding the amounts of sunshine other plants require is essential to practical gardening. Full sun is ideal for sun-loving plants like tomatoes and peppers, but shade-tolerant types like leafy greens and some herbs can do well with less direct sunshine. Every plant gets the right amount of sun thanks to the placement of the garden beds or containers, which accounts for the sun's course during the day. The interplay of light and shadow transforms into a choreography that determines the garden's health and vitality by impacting photosynthesis, growth, and the maturation of flowers and fruits.

The essential component of gardening is water, sometimes known as the "elixir of life." Plant health depends on knowing when and how much to water. While underwatering can result in wilting plants, stunted development, and decreased yields, overwatering can cause saturated soil, root rot, and nutrient leaching. Plant type, soil type, and meteorological conditions are some variables that affect how much moisture a plant needs. Watering in the morning or evening maximizes water absorption and reduces waste because these times of day have lower temperatures and less evaporation. To minimize wetting the leaves and lower the danger of infections, water can be delivered straight to the base of plants using drip irrigation, soaker hoses, or cautious hand watering.

Begun with seeds, the minuscule carriers of life, gardening starts here. Successful gardening requires understanding the plant life cycle, from seed germination to flowering and fruiting. The parameters necessary for germination differ amongst plants and include temperature, moisture content, and light levels. Before transferring seedlings into the garden, starting seeds indoors in pots—such as seed trays or peat pots—provides a controlled germination environment. Certain crops that prefer not to be disturbed while transplanting are ideal for direct sowing, which involves putting seeds directly into the soil. The beginning of the gardener's responsibility as a steward of life is growing seeds into vigorous seedlings.

Companion planting is a long-standing technique based on conventional agricultural knowledge that entails carefully matching plants to promote their growth and ward against pests. There are symbiotic interactions between some plant pairings, in which one plant repels pests that harm its companion, or one plant supplies nutrients that the other plant needs. For instance, growing beans next to corn helps the soil fix nitrogen, while putting basil near tomatoes can help discourage tomato hornworms. In addition to making the most of the available space in the garden, companion planting encourages a comprehensive and ecologically sound approach to pest control.

Even though it's sometimes seen as a tedious chore, weeding is essential to keeping a garden healthy. If weeds increase, they can swiftly take over a garden by competing with cultivated plants for nutrition, moisture, and sunlight. Frequent weeding ensures that desired plants have optimal growing conditions by preventing the depletion of resources meant for them. Mulching, or adding organic materials to the soil's surface, such as wood chips, straw, or leaves, has two benefits: it keeps the soil moist longer and inhibits weed growth. Removing weeds transforms into a contemplative activity that enables the gardener to establish a connection with the soil and actively enhance the garden's health.

The complex processes involved in pollination, an essential part of plant reproduction, highlight the interdependencies among the connections in the garden. For many plants to produce fruits and seeds, pollinators—bees, butterflies, and other insects—transfer pollen from male to female flowers. Planting a wide variety of flowering plants that give these beneficial insects nectar and pollen is the first step in creating a pollinator-friendly landscape. Companion planting can also assist pollination since some plants draw pollinators, and others ward off pests that could impede pollination. Understanding nature's delicate balance is fostered by knowing pollinators' responsibilities in the garden.

Pruning, or the deliberate removal of specific plant parts, is an artistic process that influences the garden's composition, well-being, and output. Pruning can be used to shape plants for aesthetic reasons, eliminate unhealthy or dead growth, and promote the growth of fruits and flowers. Pruning needs vary amongst plants, and timing is often critical to prevent overtaxing the plant. In addition to lowering the danger of illness, routine trimming increases air circulation and lets sunlight reach every part of the plant. Pruning with meticulous skill increases the garden's visual appeal and general vitality by creating a harmonious tapestry of shapes and hues.

One of the most essential parts of managing garden pests is awareness of how illnesses and pests reproduce. Recognizing typical pests and diseases, such as aphids, caterpillars, or fungal infections, enables the gardener to take preventative action and deal with problems when they emerge. To reduce chemical pesticides, integrated pest management, or IPM, takes a comprehensive strategy combining mechanical, biological, and cultural control techniques. One can attract beneficial insects to the garden to organically reduce pest populations, like ladybugs or predatory wasps. The secret to effective pest management is balancing limiting damage to useful creatures and the larger environment and maintaining the garden's health.

Animal Husbandry: Caring for Livestock

Animal husbandry is the practice of caring for, managing, and raising cattle. It is situated at the nexus of agriculture and stewardship. The ethical and appropriate care of domesticated animals is guided by the principles of animal husbandry, which apply to both small backyard homesteads and large farms. To develop a symbiotic relationship between humans and animals that covers the domains of nourishment, shelter, health, and ethical issues, this section explores the complexities of caring for livestock.

The supply of suitable and balanced diets is crucial for the health and welfare of animals, and it is the cornerstone of adequate animal husbandry. Different animal species have different dietary needs determined by breed, age, and intended use. Ruminants, which include sheep and cattle, do well on diets high in forages like legumes and grasses because they have the necessary fiber for healthy digestion. Conversely, a protein-rich diet is essential for poultry to sustain growth and egg production. Livestock are guaranteed access to clean water, mineral supplements, and nutrient content critical for growth, reproduction, and general health.

It is impossible to exaggerate the significance of pasture management in animal husbandry, especially for grazing animals like cattle, sheep, and goats. Rotational grazing is a technique that allows pastures to recuperate by preventing overgrazing and promoting consistent fodder use by putting animals through different pasture parts in a prearranged order. In addition to meeting the nutritional demands of cattle, well-managed pastures promote biodiversity, soil health, and erosion prevention. With rotational grazing, the natural behaviors of cattle become essential to maintaining a healthy and sustainable ecosystem, demonstrating the symbiotic relationship between animals and the soil.

Livestock can find refuge in a shelter, which protects them from the weather and offers a place to sleep and feel safe. Animal housing is designed and built differently depending on species, climate, and management techniques. Shelters such as barns, sheds, or open shelters protect against bad weather, excessive heat, and predators. Ensuring enough ventilation prevents moisture accumulation and maintains high-quality air in confined areas. In addition to making animals more comfortable, bedding items like wood shavings or straws also help with waste management. Animal housing becomes a crucial part of animal husbandry because it provides an environment favorable for expressing natural behaviors and physical safety.

In animal husbandry, health management is a complex process that includes veterinarian treatment, disease prevention, and general well-being. Immunizations, parasite management, and biosecurity protocols are the cornerstone of illness prevention. Frequent health examinations by licensed veterinarians allow for the early identification of possible problems and the use of suitable remedies. Animals with proper nutrition are more resilient overall and better able to tolerate stress and fend off illnesses. An essential component of ethical health management is the prudent use of antibiotics and other drugs, emphasizing reducing the emergence of antibiotic resistance. Livestock health is a dynamic facet of animal husbandry that necessitates ongoing attention to detail, proactive approaches, and a dedication to moral care.

Reproduction and breeding play a crucial role in animal husbandry, affecting cattle's genetic composition and yield. Selective breeding aims to improve desired characteristics within a population, such as growth rate, milk production, or disease resistance. Depending on the species and management objectives, artificial insemination or natural mating may be used in breeding programs. Making educated breeding decisions is facilitated by maintaining accurate records, which include pedigree data and reproductive history. When it comes to breeding, ethical considerations entail abstaining from methods that could endanger the health or welfare of the animals, like severe inbreeding or trait selection for undesirable qualities. Maintaining the general well-being of animals while pursuing desired features is a fine line in the responsible stewardship of animal genetics.

Beyond meeting basic needs, ethical considerations in animal husbandry include treating animals with respect and humanity throughout their lives. The Farm Animal Welfare Council developed the framework, The Five Freedoms, which outlines the essential tenets of moral animal husbandry: freedom from pain, injury, or disease; freedom from hunger and thirst; freedom to exhibit normal behavior; and freedom from fear and distress. These liberties guide the creation of moral guidelines and procedures for the management of animals. Giving animals enough room, social interaction, and opportunity to engage in their natural behaviors aligns with moral values and promotes a positive human-animal bond.

Livestock integration into agroecosystems is a prime example of sustainable animal husbandry's all-encompassing methodology. Using livestock and crops to maximize overall productivity and reduce environmental effects is known as agroecological techniques. For instance, incorporating chickens into orchards enables them to scavenge for insects and use their excrement as a natural fertilizer. Rotational grazing systems maximize soil health and feed use by migrating cattle throughout land areas. The agroecosystem's nutrient cycle is completed by incorporating livestock dung as an organic fertilizer. Sustainable animal husbandry techniques encourage healthy and regenerative interaction between animals and the environment, minimize resource usage, and prioritize the land's health.

The notion of compassionate slaughter emphasizes the moral issues in animal husbandry by accepting that an animal's life will inevitably come to an end in the agricultural system. The welfare of the animals is the priority in humane slaughter procedures, which ensure they are handled, transported, and processed with the least amount of stress and anxiety. Establishments that follow ethical standards for animal slaughter use techniques like stunning, which knocks animals out before the killing process, to minimize suffering. An appreciation of the value of a dignified and humane exit from the agricultural system and a dedication to compassion and respect is reflected in the ethical treatment of animals near the end of their life.

Backyard and small-scale animal husbandry have become popular as people seek deeper connections. To their food sources and adopt a more ecological way of living. Raising small herds of cattle in urban or suburban environments, known as urban homesteading, presents unique opportunities and problems for animal husbandry. Urban homesteaders frequently raise chickens, rabbits, and miniature goats, which can produce milk, meat, and eggs on a small scale. Factors including regional regulations, spatial limitations, and the requirement for substitute feeding and disposal methods are considered. Urban animal husbandry serves as a microcosm for the more significant ideas of ecological techniques, moral treatment, and integrating animals into various residential settings.

To sum up, animal husbandry is intricate and ever-changing, necessitating a sophisticated comprehension of the requirements, actions, and moral implications of raising animals. The concepts of animal husbandry influence the interactions between humans and the animals under their care in various ways, including nourishment and shelter, breeding, health management, and ethical treatment. The humane treatment of animals, conscientious behavior, and the incorporation of livestock into agricultural systems that emphasize environmental health and sustainability are all components of ethical livestock husbandry. We become guardians of a delicate and symbiotic relationship that goes right to the core of ethical and sustainable agriculture as we skillfully negotiate the complex dance of caring for livestock.

DIY Projects for a Self-Sufficient Homestead

To live a more self-sufficient lifestyle, people frequently look into do-it-yourself (DIY) projects that improve their homesteads' sustainability, efficiency, and usability. Homesteaders can actively participate in creating their living environments by building solar dehydrators for food preservation or raising beds for vegetable farming. This section explores a range of do-it-yourself projects that can help make a self-sufficient farm. These projects cover topics including food production, energy efficiency, water management, and resilience in general. These initiatives promote independence and the spirit of ingenuity and sustainability that characterizes the self-sufficient homesteading way of life.

Building raised beds for gardening is one of the core do-it-yourself tasks for a self-sufficient homestead. Increased soil drainage, greater control over soil quality, and a lower chance of soil compaction are benefits of raised beds. With resources like untreated lumber, salvaged pallets, or even repurposed items like old tires, building raised beds can be a reasonably easy yet impactful endeavor. Raised beds can be customized to meet the needs of the cultivated crops and the space constraints. This do-it-yourself project offers a helpful way to grow food efficiently and gives the homestead's landscaping a unique touch.

Another do-it-yourself project that adheres to the values of environmental stewardship and self-sufficiency is composting systems. Kitchen leftovers, yard waste, and other organic items can be composted to create nutrient-rich compost, an excellent soil supplement for garden beds. You can use various materials to build a compost bin or pile, such as wire mesh, wooden pallets, or recycled containers. By closing the nutrient loop on the farm and converting organic matter into an accessible and sustainable fertilizer supply, the do-it-yourself composting project minimizes household waste and improves soil health. Composting turns into a cyclical process that strengthens the homestead ecology and benefits the garden.

Projects that collect and store water are essential to guaranteeing a homestead's self-sufficient water supply, particularly in areas with erratic rainfall. Rainwater from roofs can be managed by do-it-yourself rainwater harvesting systems and directed into storage tanks or cisterns. Installing gutters, downspouts, and a filtration system may be necessary to create a rainwater collecting setup that guarantees the water collected is clean and suitable for usage. DIY water management projects also involve building swales and berms to catch and slow down rainwater runoff, promote absorption into the soil, and lessen erosion. These programs support the sustainable use and conservation of this priceless resource and offer a reliable water source.

Building a solar dehydrator exemplifies how inventive and resourceful self-sufficient homesteaders can be. Solar dehydrators use solar energy instead of electricity to preserve fruits, vegetables, and herbs. Constructing a solar dehydrator out of corrugated metal, plastic, glass, and wood is possible. Typically, the design consists of slatted trays for the produce, a reflective surface to optimize solar exposure, and sufficient ventilation to ensure adequate drying. With this do-it-yourself project, homesteaders may increase the shelf life of their harvest, cut down on food waste, and develop a sustainable food preservation technique that adheres to self-sufficiency ideals.

Building a DIY chicken coop is A practical project incorporating animal husbandry into the self-sufficient household. Homesteaders frequently raise chickens for meat and eggs, and creating a chicken coop is essential to giving the flock a secure and comfortable environment. Designs for DIY chicken coops can be as basic as A-frame buildings or as complex as multi-story buildings with built-in nesting boxes. Using recycled materials gives the project a more sustainable feel. Examples of these resources are used pallets and recovered lumber. Since the chickens provide vital manure for garden fertility in addition to eggs and meat, the DIY chicken coop forms a critical component of the homestead's food production system.

Regarding energy efficiency, do-it-yourself solar panel installations are the perfect example of a homestead's dedication to renewable energy sources. Sunlight is converted into electricity by solar panels, offering a sustainable and clean power source for various home requirements. Although hiring a professional installer is an option, many homesteaders decide to do their installation to save money and keep a hands-on relationship with their energy system. Installing solar panels on roofs or ground and connecting them to batteries and inverters for energy storage are the components of do-it-yourself solar energy projects. These programs not only lessen the homestead's dependency on grid electricity but also strengthen and sustain its energy infrastructure.

Handcrafted wood-fired ovens enable baking bread, pizzas, and other baked items, a valuable and entertaining addition to a self-sufficient farm. Constructing a wood-fired oven blends aspects of building, design, and cooking arts into a satisfying project. According to the builder's abilities and tastes, DIY oven ideas can be as basic as cob or clay constructions or as complex as brick ovens. Using fuel from the homestead, the oven becomes the center of attention for outdoor cooking, providing an off-grid and sustainable culinary experience. This do-it-yourself project improves self-sufficiency and infuses the farm lifestyle with a hint of traditional craftsmanship.

Hugelkultur beds made at home provide a regenerative and sustainable farming option for homesteaders looking to implement permaculture concepts into their landscape. Creating raised beds full of organic materials, branches, and decaying wood is called hugelkultur. The rotting wood retains moisture and nutrients for the roots of plants, acting as a sponge. Logs, branches, leaves, and dirt can be layered to create hugelkultur beds. This do-it-yourself effort not only turns organic waste into a valuable resource but also, in the long run, increases soil resilience and fertility. Hugelkultur beds serve as a working illustration of how to replicate natural processes to increase homestead productivity.

Rain barrel systems are a simple, environmentally responsible do-it-yourself project that may be used to collect and store rainwater for garden irrigation. Building a rain barrel system entails repurposing sizable containers, like plastic drums or food-grade barrels, to catch rainwater from downspouts. A spigot and an overflow system are two straightforward additions that make using the collected rainwater for irrigating plants simple. Installing a rain barrel yourself not only saves water but also lessens dependency on public water sources. This initiative contributes to a more resilient homestead ecosystem by adhering to sustainability, self-sufficiency, and water conservation concepts.

Building a homemade root cellar offers a way to store fruits and vegetables. and keeps its freshness without electricity. Root cellars provide a regulated environment for long-term storage by exploiting the earth's inherent cooling. Excavation, insulation, and ventilation strategies are necessary while building a root cellar to maintain ideal humidity and temperature levels. Homesteaders may increase the shelf life of their harvest with this do-it-yourself project, which lessens the need for refrigeration and encourages a more environmentally friendly method of food preservation. The self-sufficient homestead gains a valuable and timeless element in the root cellar that unites historical customs with contemporary demands.

CHAPTER IV

Growing Your Own Food

Establishing a Productive Vegetable Garden

Growing a successful vegetable garden can lead to abundant harvests, a wealth of nutrients, and a close relationship with the natural cycles. Starting a vegetable garden is a fulfilling undertaking, whether the motivation is to grow food, indulge in a gardening hobby, or adopt an independent way of life. This section examines the essential components of developing a fruitful vegetable garden: crop selection, soil preparation, planting methods, and continuous upkeep. By being thoroughly aware of the elements that contribute to a successful vegetable garden, anyone can turn a plot of land into a productive source of locally grown food, enjoying access to fresh, tasty, and nourishing fruits and vegetables.

The quality of the soil is the cornerstone of any successful vegetable garden. The garden's lifeblood is the soil, which offers vital nutrients, air, and a surface on which plant roots can attach and spread. It is essential to evaluate the structure and content of the soil before planting. Accessible via garden centers or agricultural extension organizations, soil testing kits offer significant insights regarding pH balance and nutrient levels. To increase soil fertility, additions like compost, well-rotted manure, or organic matter can be added based on the findings. Well-draining soil is essential to prevent soggy roots and guarantee that oxygen reaches plant roots for optimum growth. Soil preparation becomes a systematic and fundamental stage in establishing the framework for a successful and fruitful food garden.

The choice of crops is essential to a vegetable garden's success. Several variables influence crop selection, including growing season, climate, available area, and individual preferences. Inexperienced gardeners should begin with a variety of climate-appropriate, low-maintenance veggies. Tomatoes, peppers, lettuce, carrots, and herbs are famous for novices. When designing the garden's layout, it is crucial to comprehend each crop's growing requirements and habits. One important factor to consider is companion planting, which is the deliberate placement of crops to promote development and ward against pests. For instance, growing basil close to tomatoes can help ward off harmful pests. The foundation for a pleasant and fruitful plant interaction in the vegetable garden is laid by careful crop selection.

Vertical space use, spacing, and arrangement must be considered when designing the garden's plan. Plants spaced properly provide for sufficient airflow, sunshine penetration, and simplicity of maintenance while preventing congestion. The layout of crops inside garden beds is guided by companion planting concepts, which consider the beneficial or harmful interactions between different plant species. For vining crops like beans or cucumbers, maximizing growing areas can be achieved by utilizing vertical space, such as trellises or stakes. A thoughtful design makes the most of the available space and enhances the vegetable garden's overall appeal, resulting in a welcoming and valuable outdoor area.

One crucial element that significantly affects a vegetable garden's performance is when it is planted. It is helpful to know the local climate when to expect frost, and the requirements unique to each crop when deciding when to plant. Warm-season crops, like tomatoes and peppers, enjoy the warmth of late spring and summer, while cool-season crops, like spinach and peas, flourish in the colder temps of spring and fall. Using seed trays or pots to start seeds indoors enables early germination and robust seedling development before transplanting them into the garden. Some crops do better with direct seeding, which involves sowing seeds straight into the ground; these crops would like to avoid disturbing their roots when transplanting. Every crop is provided with the best possible conditions for germination, growth, and eventual harvest thanks to the skill of timing.

In the vegetable garden, healthy and robust plants are established with the help of proper planting procedures. Handling seedlings carefully while transplanting them is essential, limiting root disruption and ensuring the soil sticks to the roots. A successful transplant is facilitated by excavating planting holes with the correct depth and spacing and by enriching the soil with compost or organic matter. Watering newly planted seedlings lessens transplant shock and helps the soil around the roots settle. Seeds are sown at the suggested depth when direct seeding, covered with soil and given enough moisture to facilitate germination. Mulching, or the topsoil dressing with organic materials like wood chips or straw, helps control temperature, weed growth, and moisture retention. Planting becomes a thoughtful and intentional procedure that paves the way for the food garden's expansion and improvement.

Growing a successful vegetable garden requires constant attention to detail and upkeep. Watering is one of the most critical aspects of gardening maintenance, and healthy plants depend on regular and sufficient moisture. The kind of soil, the needs of each crop, and the weather all affect how often and how much water is needed. Watering plants in the morning or evening reduces water evaporation and the risk of fungal diseases. Mulching around plants helps suppress weed growth and retain water. Consistently checking for indications of pests or illnesses facilitates prompt action, be it via organic pesticides, natural therapies, or companion planting techniques. Eliminating undesirable plants or weeds guarantees that resources go toward the grown crops and lessens competition for sunshine and nutrients. Certain crops with sprawling or vining growth patterns may require staking or pruning. Maintaining the vegetable garden becomes a dynamic and adaptable technique that is aware of the changing demands of the

Vegetation and the surroundings. Fermentation is crucial to keep the soil fertile and encourage plant growth. The slow-releasing nutrients in compost and well-rotted manure are examples of organic fertilizers. Synthetic fertilizers can be used only by the suggested timing and rates. Fertilizer application is guided by crop-specific requirements that are impacted by factors such as plant growth stage and soil nutrient levels. Natural soil fertility can be increased by pairing nitrogen-fixing plants, like legumes, with companion planting. Moreover, crop rotation—planting various crops one after the other to keep pests and diseases from building up—contributes to the soil's long-term health. The management of vegetable gardens involves applying sophisticated and flexible fertilization techniques that strive to balance the provision of vital nutrients and the advancement of soil sustainability.

Fruit Orchards and Berry Bushes

Planting berry bushes and fruit orchards is an adventure into a world of horticultural diversity, where nature's abundance presents itself in a kaleidoscope of hues, tastes, and nutrient density. Fruit-bearing trees and bushes can be grown in backyards or on larger agricultural plots, and they provide a variety of advantages, such as improved biodiversity, tasty, fresh products, and support for a healthy ecosystem. This section delves into the complexities of creating and caring for berry bushes and fruit orchards, examining essential factors like site selection, types of trees and bushes, pruning methods, and sustainable practices that support the success of these flourishing orchards.

The first step in creating a thriving orchard or berry patch is choosing a site. The appropriateness of the site, which takes into account elements like climate, drainage, soil composition, and sunshine exposure, is critical to the success of fruit growing. Fruit trees, such as those that provide apples, peaches, and cherries, do best in areas that receive full sun for a considerable amount of the day. Soil with good drainage is essential for avoiding soggy roots and lowering the likelihood of illnesses. To maximize fertility, decisions about soil amendments are informed by the results of a soil test, which evaluates pH and nutrient levels. By choosing a location with adequate air circulation, fungal diseases are less likely to occur, improving the tree's general health. Site-specific elements are carefully considered to ensure that the berry patch or orchard is positioned for productivity and durability.

Creating a dynamic and plentiful fruit landscape largely depends on the diversity of tree and bush kinds. The selection of fruit tree kinds for an orchard should consider various aspects, including disease resistance, compatibility with pollination, and chilling requirements. Depending on the species and variety, fruit trees require varying amounts of winter cold hours to break dormancy.

A longer time of active development in the orchard is ensured by choosing cultivars with overlapping chilling hours. Fruit set depends on pollination compatibility because some kinds need to be cross-pollinated with compatible mates to produce the most fruit. Varieties resistant to diseases and common pests are bred to make an orchard more low-maintenance and sustainable. A consistent yield is guaranteed throughout the growing season by combining early, mid-, and late-season cultivars. One must choose berry bushes that are compatible with the local climate. For example, blueberries should be planted in acidic soils, while raspberries should be planted in well-drained areas. Careful selection of tree and shrub varieties promotes resilience and adaptability to changing environmental conditions in addition to diversity.

It becomes clear that pruning is a creative and necessary technique for maintaining berry bushes and food orchards. Pruning has several functions, including controlling fruit output, fostering ventilation, reshaping the tree or bush, and warding off disease. Trees in orchards can be easily managed and harvested since trimming affects the form and structure of the trees. Commonly used training methods are either open-center or central-leader, which have advantages about air circulation and sunshine penetration. Annual pruning encourages the growth of new fruiting wood, eliminates sick or dead wood, and reroutes growth to desirable branches. Pruning requires careful planning. Dormant-season pruning, which is usually done in late winter or early spring, is a widespread technique. Blackberry and raspberry bushes, for example, require pruning that includes pulling off old canes, thinning out dense growth, and promoting the emergence of robust lateral shoots. In addition to improving the orchard's aesthetic appeal, proper pruning supports the general health and productivity of trees and bushes that provide fruit.

The lifetime and ecological balance of berry patches and fruit orchards depend on adopting sustainable techniques. Cultural practices, beneficial insects, and biological control techniques precede chemical interventions in integrated pest management (IPM) systems. IPM includes employing natural predators to manage pest populations, setting up pheromone traps, and conducting routine pest monitoring. One aspect of integrated pest management (IPM) is the selective application of pesticides only when necessary and with care for non-target organisms.

Organic orchard management adheres to environmental stewardship and sustainability ideals by avoiding synthetic pesticides and fertilizers. Including cover crops such as legumes or clover improves soil fertility, keeps weeds at bay, and fosters a diversified environment. Mulching around berry bushes and fruit trees helps to control temperature, retain soil moisture, and inhibit the growth of weeds. Techniques for conserving water, such as rainwater collection and drip irrigation, enhance resource efficiency. In the orchard and around berry patches, growing native plants or wildflowers attracts pollinators, increases biodiversity, and builds ecosystem resilience. Fruit farming becomes a regenerative and ecologically sensitive enterprise where the values of caring for the land and its people are prioritized when sustainable techniques are implemented.

Pollination is an exciting and essential part of growing fruits, which is a complicated process combining insects, wind, and plant biology. Pollinators like bees are necessary for fruit to set successfully on many fruit trees—such as those that grow cherries, pears, and apples. Adequate pollination requires a variety of healthy pollinator populations, such as native bees, honeybees, and other insects. Having blooming plants available, either

Provides a home and habitat for pollinators inside the orchard or nearby areas. The success of cross-pollination is influenced by the time of fruit types' blooms, underscoring the significance of choosing suitable kinds within the orchard. Certain berry bushes require cross-pollination to produce fruit, but others can be self-pollinating. Orchard planning is aided by knowledge of the particular pollination needs of berry bushes and fruit trees, which encourages maximum fruit output. The complex dance of pollination emphasizes how ecological diversity and interdependence enable agricultural abundance in the natural world.

The sustainability of cultivation practices, overall health, and fruit quality are all impacted by effective water management, which is an essential part of maintaining berry patches and fruit orchards. Consistent and sufficient hydration is necessary for fruit trees and bushes, particularly during crucial phases like blossoming, fruit development, and dry spells. Drip irrigation systems minimize water waste and lower the risk of fungal infections linked to overhead watering by providing water directly to the root zone. Weather-based irrigation controllers or soil moisture sensors help maximize water utilization by modifying irrigation schedules in response to environmental circumstances. Mulching around shrubs and trees helps to control temperature, prevent weed growth, and preserve soil moisture. Rainwater harvesting systems decrease dependency on municipal water supplies by collecting and storing rainwater for later use.

Water conservation techniques support a more robust and resource-efficient orchard ecosystem by supporting sustainable water management principles and improving the health of fruit-bearing plants.

Maximizing Space with Container Gardening

Within the urban and small-space gardening domain, where outdoor space is frequently scarce, container gardening is a flexible and effective means of growing plants, flowers, and food. Container gardening provides a blank canvas for creative gardening, allowing people to turn small spaces into thriving green havens, whether they are on balconies, patios, rooftops, or windowsills. The art and science of container gardening are examined in this section, which also covers essential topics, including plant selection, soil composition, container selection, and maintenance techniques. Gardening enthusiasts may make the most of their space, bring nature within, and experience horticultural joy by utilizing containers to their full potential.

The first stage in container gardening is choosing the appropriate containers, which affect the plants' development, health, and visual attractiveness. Terracotta, plastic, wood, and metal are just a few materials used to make containers; each has pros and problems. For example, terracotta pots are renowned for their permeability, allowing air to reach the plant roots and avoiding soggy soil. Plastic containers work well for various plant species since they are lightweight and hold moisture efficiently. Wooden receptacles offer a rustic and natural aesthetic, but to keep them from rotting, you must line them and choose rot-resistant wood. Although sturdy, metal containers can absorb heat, impacting soil temperature and necessitating insulation in warm areas. Size is also essential; bigger pots offer more soil volume and stability, promoting plant growth. The choice of containers becomes a deliberate and critical part of the gardening process, influencing the small-space oasis's usability and aesthetic appeal.

Plant roots' nutrients, aeration, and drainage depend primarily on the soil composition of containers. Because container plants rely entirely on the soil in their small growing environment, choosing a suitable soil is essential. A premium potting mix specially designed for container gardening guarantees an even distribution of organic matter, perlite, vermiculite, and other nutrients. Potting mixes give plants the vital nutrients to flourish, encourage proper drainage, and guard against compaction. To improve soil fertility and water retention, gardeners can add organic matter, such as compost, to the potting mix. Maintaining ideal growing conditions inside the container is facilitated by routinely checking the moisture content of the soil and modifying irrigation techniques. Creating the perfect soil composition in containers becomes a skill that establishes the foundation for thriving and healthy plant life.

With container gardening, you may grow various plants, including vegetables, herbs, ornamentals, and small fruit trees. Several variables, including climate, sunlight availability, and container size, determine the plants chosen. Blooming annuals like petunias, marigolds, or geraniums give splashes of color and visual appeal to sunny balconies or patios. Herbs like basil, mint, and rosemary grow well in containers, adding a vibrant taste to food preparations. Growing fresh, homegrown produce in an urban setting is doable, thanks to the development of container gardening for vegetables like lettuce, tomatoes, and peppers. Small spaces are enhanced by the addition of miniature citrus or apple trees, sometimes known as dwarf or patio fruit trees. Cacti and succulents are great options for sunny windowsills because of their low maintenance requirements and water efficiency. Because there are so many plant options, container gardeners may create a unique and varied green area in a small space.

Container gardening requires more thoughtful moisture management due to the small space and restricted soil volume. This means that watering procedures must be closely monitored. The kind of plants, the type of container, and the weather all affect how often and how much watering is necessary. Terracotta and unglazed ceramic pots, in particular, tend to dry up faster than plastic or metal containers and need to be watered more frequently. Using saucers or trays underneath pots can help retain excess water, shield surfaces from water damage, and give plants a place to collect water between waterings. Watering decisions are guided by routinely checking soil moisture, either by feeling the top inch of soil or using a moisture meter. Water evaporation and plant stress during the day's heat decrease when plants are watered in the morning or the evening. It's crucial to strike the correct balance when watering containers because overdoing it can cause root rot and other problems. Ensuring that plants receive the necessary moisture for optimal growth, watering becomes an intuitive and responsive art.

In container gardening, fertilization is essential since it makes up for the restricted amount of nutrients in the containers. Because water removes nutrients from the soil with every irrigation, container plants depend on the gardener to supply vital nutrients. For container plants, water-soluble fertilizers provide an easy and efficient method of delivering nutrients during the growing season. When added to the potting mix or sprayed on the soil's surface, slow-release fertilizers offer a consistent

And sustained source of nutrients. Organic fertilizers, such as compost or well-rotted manure, can be regularly added to the soil to improve fertility. Fertilization procedures are adjusted based on routine monitoring for indicators of nutritional inadequacies, such as yellowing leaves or stunted development. Fertilizer selection becomes a delicate balancing act that guarantees container plants get the nutrients they need for healthy growth without going overboard and possibly causing harm.

Container plants require regular pruning and grooming to keep their shape, encourage airflow, and avoid crowding. Pruning promotes the growth of a bushier and more compact form and helps regulate the size of plants, especially in containers with limited space. Removing spent flowers, or deadheading, extends the blooming season and focuses energy on new growth. Reducing the amount of overgrown foliage in containers improves ventilation and lowers the possibility of fungal illnesses. Cleaning and trimming fading or damaged leaves helps keep container plants looking neat and colorful. Pruning and grooming transform the container garden into an aesthetically beautiful and well-kept area, embracing horticultural art.

In container gardening, where plants are in close quarters, and diseases can spread quickly, protection from pests and diseases is essential. Early intervention is possible when pests like aphids, spider mites, or caterpillars are regularly observed for signs of infestation. Certain pests can be managed with insecticidal soaps or neem oil, well-known for their efficiency and little adverse environmental effects. Container gardens are further protected by companion planting, the deliberate positioning of plants that deter pests or draw beneficial insects. Prune trees appropriately, space them apart, and apply fungicidal treatments to reduce the spread of fungal diseases exacerbated by high humidity and inadequate air circulation. Before adding new plants to the container garden, quarantine them to stop the spread of illnesses or pests. Container gardens are kept healthy and pest-free through proactive methods and vigilant monitoring, which enables plants to flourish in their small but well-maintained areas.

CHAPTER V

Raising Happy and Healthy Livestock

Choosing the Right Livestock for Your Space

Raising livestock is an endeavor that requires much thought and preparation before beginning. No matter how big or tiny your backyard is, choosing the correct kind of livestock is an important choice that affects the animals' welfare and the outcome of your project. This section explores the complexities of selecting livestock, including the amount of land needed, local laws, and the requirements of individual animals. Prospective livestock keepers can establish a happy atmosphere where animals and humans thrive by knowing the subtleties of choosing the correct cattle for your space.

The quantity of available space is the primary factor when selecting animals. How big your land is will determine what kind and how many animals you can rear ethically and responsibly. More spacious rural properties could suit larger animals like sheep, goats, or cattle. These animals need a lot of grazing pasture to meet their nutritional needs and maintain their well-being. People who live in suburban backyards or on smaller pieces of land might find that chickens, rabbits, or miniature goats are better choices. Complying with local standards, maintaining a healthy environment, and preventing overcrowding depends on knowing how much room each variety of cattle needs.

Considering zoning laws and local regulations is crucial when deciding whether to raise animals on your land. The rules regarding the types and number of animals allowed, and the construction of animal enclosures and shelters vary from place to place. Researching and adhering to these rules is essential to avoid legal issues and maintain good relations with local government and neighbors. Some towns may prohibit keeping larger animals in residential areas, making choosing livestock that comply with local laws essential. By taking the time to understand and follow these regulations, prospective livestock keepers can ensure a smooth and lawful integration of animals into their homes. This understanding can instill a sense of responsibility, knowing they abide by the law and respect their community's standards.

Understanding various livestock species' unique requirements and traits is critical to making informed decisions. Each animal type has different housing, feeding, and medical care needs. For instance, cattle require large grazing areas, strong fences, and protection from harsh weather. Due to their browsing habits, goats may need secure fencing to prevent them from escaping. Poultry like chickens and ducks need suitable housing for roosting and nesting and protection from predators. Rabbits thrive in well-ventilated enclosures with ample space for running around. Miniature or' micro' livestock breeds, which offer the appeal of larger animals in a more compact form, are increasingly popular in urban and small-scale settings. These breeds—mini goats or little pigs—retain many charming traits of their full-sized counterparts while often requiring less space and resources. By understanding the unique needs and characteristics of each type of livestock, prospective keepers can ensure the animals' welfare is prioritized, and their care aligns with their natural tendencies. This knowledge can lead to a sense of accomplishment, knowing that the livestock's wellbeing is secured through informed decisions.

The purpose of raising livestock is a vital part of the decision-making process. Some people may be interested in producing dairy products or fiber, while others may want to raise animals for meat. Still, others might keep animals as pets or for educational purposes. The choice of species and breeds, as well as the management techniques used, are influenced by these intended purposes. For instance, those interested in meat production might choose breeds known for their high-quality meat and efficient feed conversion. Those interested in dairy farming might prefer dairy goats or small cows known for their high milk yield. Fiber enthusiasts might opt for alpacas or Angora rabbits. Understanding the intended purpose helps align livestock-raising goals with the practical aspects of their upkeep and management. This alignment can bring a sense of satisfaction, knowing that the chosen livestock aligns with their goals and can be managed effectively.

The climate and environmental factors are essential in deciding which cattle are appropriate for a particular area. Because different animals can tolerate different temperatures, it is important to tailor an animal's housing and care to the climate in which it lives. Heat-tolerant breeds are more suited for warmer climes, whereas cold-hardy breeds might be more appropriate for places with severe winters. The animals' well-being depends on wellbeing enough cover and defense against adverse weather, such as wind, rain, or heat. It is also essential to have access to clean water and a diet that is adequate for the area's forage and resources. People may build a robust and sustainable system that supports the health and vigor of the animals by matching the livestock they choose with the local natural circumstances.

The degree of engagement and dedication people can devote to cattle farming is an important consideration when making decisions. Consistent care, attention, and wellbeing are necessary for livestock. Responsible animal husbandry requires frequent veterinarian care, cleaning, and feeding. The time and effort needed for handling, training, and interacting with the animals should also be considered. Certain animals, like goats and pigs, are noted for their intelligence and can need greater mental and social stimulation. Some animals, like rabbits or chickens, might only need basic upkeep. When potential livestock keepers know the time commitment necessary, they can make decisions that fit their availability and lifestyle.

A practical factor to consider when integrating cattle into a property is compatibility with the land's intended or current use. Whatever the other land use, livestock should work in harmony with it rather than against it, be it landscaping, gardening, or outdoor pleasure, and comprehending the effects of cattle on flora, soil, and additional landscape components aids in the development and execution of sustainable land management techniques. Rotational grazing systems, for instance, can ensure a peaceful coexistence between cattle and the environment by preventing overgrazing and promoting soil health. Making plans for waste management—like turning manure into fertilizer by composting it—helps create a closed-loop system that increases the operation's sustainability. People can design integrated, holistic living environments that support the wellbeing of animawellbeingmans by considering the compatibility of livestock with current land uses.

The availability of appropriate veterinary care, immunizations, and preventive measures is essential for the health and welfare of cattle. Effective disease prevention and management require understanding the needs and common health problems of many species. Vaccinations, deworming procedures, and routine veterinarian examinations all contribute to the general wellbeing and lifewellbeinghe animals. Potential health problems can be identified early on by monitoring livestock's behavior, appetite, and physical state. Quarantine for newly acquired animals aids in preventing the spread of illness inside the current flock or herd. Enough food, uncontaminated water, and appropriate housing contribute to the animals' wellbeing. A healwellbeingsilient herd or flock is guaranteed by taking a proactive and preventative approach to animal health care.

Building Coops and Shelters

Building coops and other housing for livestock is an essential part of ethical animal husbandry, guaranteeing the health, protection, and comfort of the creatures in one's charge. These buildings' layout and architecture, whether used to house goats, chickens, rabbits, or other livestock, are essential to establishing a safe and comfortable atmosphere. This section examines the ideas and factors of creating coops and shelters, covering everything from material selection and architectural elements to incorporating insulation and ventilation. Through comprehension of the fundamental components of building, people can build sturdy, long-lasting shelters that enhance the well-being of their animals.

The choice of materials used to construct coops and shelters is crucial since it affects the finished structure's utility, durability, and structural integrity. Materials should be chosen according to the demands and behaviors of various livestock. Metal or wood are common lightweight, weather-resistant materials used for poultry, such as hens or ducks. In addition to being aesthetically beautiful and offering natural insulation, wood may need routine upkeep to avoid decay. Conversely, metal is easy to clean and long-lasting, but it might need to be insulated in freezing weather. Sturdy materials, such as pressure-treated wood or metal structures, are necessary to support the weight and movement of larger animals like sheep or goats. The selection of materials is guided by an understanding of the unique requirements of each variety of livestock, ensuring that the materials meet the demands of the animals as well as the climate in the area.

Coops and shelters should be designed with the individual behaviors of the animals inside them, as well as functionality and ease of upkeep. Sufficient space is essential to avoid crowding, permit organic activities, and make cleaning easier. A chicken coop should, for instance, have enough room for roosting, nesting boxes, and places to take dust baths. Feeding stations, climbing platforms, and ample room for socializing are all possible features of goat shelters. Another important design aspect is ventilation, which helps control temperature, prevent moisture buildup, and lessen odors. Vents, windows, or louvered openings let the shelter's interior air circulation function properly. The selection of flooring materials should be guided by factors such as animal comfort, ease of cleaning, and insulating qualities. Carefully incorporating design features guarantees that shelters and coops serve livestock's practical needs while improving their general well-being.

Strategic issues that affect the animals and the surrounding environment include the orientation and placement of coops and shelters within the terrain. Proper orientation can improve the shelter's usability and comfort by utilizing natural features like sunshine, wind direction, and topography. By positioning the coop such that the entrance faces away from the direction of the prevailing winds, you may prevent drafts and maintain a warmer, cozier inside. Making the most of the animals' exposure to sunshine helps control their circadian cycle, which benefits their general health. Strategically positioned shelters optimize available space and reduce their adverse effects on the surrounding environment. Shelters can be placed next to trees or existing windbreaks for extra shade and protection. The way that coops and shelters are incorporated into the surrounding environment shows a thoughtful strategy that considers the requirements of the animals and the natural surroundings.

An essential component of coop and shelter design, ventilation affects temperature control, air quality, and the animals' general comfort. A healthier and more comfortable atmosphere is produced by proper ventilation, which also helps to eliminate moisture, stale air, and smells. The design should include openings like windows, vents, or ridge vents to provide unrestricted air exchange. Proper ventilation is essential to prevent respiratory hazards in small areas where waste can accumulate and cause ammonia accumulation, such as chicken coops or rabbit hutches. Ventilation and insulation must be balanced to avoid drafts and stay comfortable in colder climates. Seasonal modifications based on weather conditions are possible using moveable windows or vents. By lowering humidity, promoting respiratory health, and reducing the chance of heat stress, ventilation considerations improve the general well-being of cattle.

For coops and shelters to be thermally comfortable, insulation is essential, especially in areas with harsh winters. Maintaining interior temperatures within an animal's comfortable range is made possible by proper insulation. Insulation lowers the risk of frostbite and other cold-related problems in colder climates by preventing drafts and trapping the heat the animals produce. Fiberglass, foam board, and natural materials like hay or straw are common materials used as insulation. Reflective insulation and light-colored roofing materials can help block sunlight and lessen heat absorption in hotter regions. In addition to ensuring a more stable and comfortable atmosphere, insulating the floor, walls, and roof increases energy efficiency. The selection and application of insulation are guided by knowledge of the local environment and seasonal fluctuations, resulting in shelters that provide animals with year-round comfort.

Practical factors like accessibility and ease of maintenance impact livestock's day-to-day care and management. Routine chores like feeding, cleaning, and health inspections should be made more accessible for coops and shelters. Sufficient entry points, like doors or hatches, facilitate access to every part of the shelter, guaranteeing that every region is noticed when cleaning or inspecting. Concrete, gravel, or detachable trays for trash collection are easy-to-maintain and durable flooring materials. Including places for machinery, bedding, or feed storage improves productivity and structure. Water collection is prevented by proper drainage features, which lowers the possibility of muck, odors, and possible health problems. Caretakers' ergonomic demands should be considered in the design to encourage a comfortable and effective workflow. The general longevity and functionality of coops and shelters are enhanced by accessibility and ease of maintenance, guaranteeing a smooth and pleasurable experience for livestock keepers and their animals.

Security measures are crucial when designing coops and shelters to protect cattle from predators and threats. The threats associated with foxes, raccoons, prey-seeking birds, and larger predators like coyotes and bears may differ depending on the location. A fence with the right height and mesh size acts as the main line of protection against predators living on the ground. To safeguard chickens from raptors, coverings or netting may be required for aerial hazards. Coop doors and windows should be safe and locked to avoid unwanted access. Because certain predators may find it challenging to access elevated regions, elevated roosting spots or platforms for more miniature cattle offer an extra layer of security—frequent examinations of the structural components and perimeter aid in locating and addressing possible weaknesses. Security measures are crucial in creating a secure and protected environment where animals can flourish without the continual fear of predation.

Sustainable Practices in Animal Care

The care and handling of animals is only one area in which sustainability concepts have crossed conventional borders and become ingrained in daily life. Sustainable methods of animal care take into account the effects of these methods on the environment, society, and economy, in addition to putting the welfare of the animals first. The many facets of sustainable animal care are examined in this section, covering topics like nutrition, waste management, ethical issues, and the incorporation of regenerative approaches. People may promote a positive human-animal relationship and help achieve the larger objective of building a more resilient and ecologically balanced world by adopting sustainable practices in animal care.

Sustainable animal care is based on ethical principles, which emphasize treating animals humanely and respecting their inherent worth. The cornerstones of ethical animal care include giving animals enough room, nutritious food, and access to clean water. Beyond the fundamentals, sustainable methods entail establishing habitats that permit animals to exhibit their natural behaviors, enhancing their mental and physical health. For example, larger animals like goats or sheep benefit from areas that allow for grazing, climbing, and social interactions, while poultry should have possibilities for dust bathing, roosting, and foraging. Sustainable animal care ethics support avoiding procedures that injure or stress animals needlessly, such as cruel confinement or overpopulation. Our dedication to ethical treatment fosters a sense of duty and compassion for the animals in our care, which acknowledges their uniqueness and agency within the larger ecosystem.

To address the environmental effects of animal husbandry techniques, waste management is a crucial component of sustainable animal care. Livestock produce various waste products, such as bedding materials, dung, and uneaten feed. Efficient use and recycling of these byproducts are critical components of sustainable approaches to reduce their environmental impact. Composting manure, a rich source of nutrients makes it an organic fertilizer that improves soil fertility and health for crops. Rotational grazing systems for larger livestock promote equal manure distribution, minimizing nutrient imbalances and soil degradation.

Furthermore, bedding materials such as wood shavings or straws can be added to compost piles or used as mulch. Sustainable animal care decreases its adverse effects on the environment. It builds closed-loop systems that improve the ecosystem's health by implementing methods that turn waste into valuable resources.

Sustainable animal care relies heavily on nutrition, which includes factors like feed mix, source, and production's environmental impact. Sustainable animal diets give preference to feed that is seasonal, locally obtained, and, if feasible, organic. The environmental impact of feed production can be reduced, and biodiversity can be enhanced by reducing the use of monoculture crops and introducing a variety of forage or pasture sources. Using pasture-based systems for livestock, such as ruminants, minimizes the requirement for substantial grain feeding while still being in line with their natural grazing patterns. Sustainable fish feed solutions that reduce dependency on wild-caught fishmeal can be incorporated into aquaculture methods. The environmental effect of producing traditional feed can also be decreased using alternative protein sources, including diets made from plants or insects. In addition to promoting the animals' health and vigor, sustainable nutrition tackles the broader environmental effects of traditional feed production methods.

Beyond sustainability, regenerative methods of animal care actively contribute to the improvement and restoration of ecosystems. A regenerative technique called rotational grazing allows grazed regions to rest and recuperate by carefully managing the movement of cattle to new paddocks. This technique fosters soil health, biodiversity, and carbon sequestration by imitating the migratory patterns of natural herbivores. Silvopasture, an integrated practice that combines livestock, forage, and trees, improves landscape productivity and ecological resilience. Animals can get shade from trees, which also enhances microclimates and helps sequester carbon. To promote a mutually beneficial relationship between livestock and the environment, regenerative approaches in animal care prioritize the restoration of damaged landscapes. Sustainable animal care becomes a catalyst for good environmental change by actively taking part in ecosystem restoration.

When making decisions, holistic management, a regenerative approach, considers how interconnected ecological, social, and economic concerns are. It places a strong emphasis on flexible and adaptable management techniques that take into account the intricacy of natural systems. Holistic management in animal care is careful planning that considers the animals' requirements, objectives for land regeneration, and the health of the surrounding ecosystems. For instance, well-considered grazing plans consider the seasonality of fodder growth, the nutritional needs of the animals, and the necessity of rest intervals to avoid overgrazing. The social and financial facets of animal care, such as community involvement, ethical labor standards, and the operation's financial stability, are also considered by holistic management techniques. Sustainable animal care has become a dynamic and adaptable practice that embraces holistic approaches and recognizes the complexity and interconnection of natural and human systems.

Sustainable practices in animal care are promoted and acknowledged in part by adopting animal welfare standards and certification schemes. These standards include information on housing, feeding, veterinary care, handling techniques, and other ethical and humane treatment requirements for animals. Customers may pick and support products made from ethically and sustainably managed animal businesses transparently and verifiable by participating in certification programs, such as those started by the American Humane Association or the Certified Humane label. These initiatives provide reassurance to consumers who place a high priority on animal welfare by entailing frequent and thorough audits and assessments to verify compliance with specified criteria. By offering a foundation for morally and responsibly caring for animals, incorporating these standards and certifications supports the larger objectives of sustainable animal care.

Outreach and educational programs are essential for advancing environmentally friendly methods of animal care. Educational programs enable people to make educated decisions by increasing their understanding of the effects of various animal husbandry practices on the environment, ethics, and health. Outreach initiatives can be directed at producers and consumers to promote a shared awareness of the relationship between animal welfare and more general sustainability objectives. The application of sustainable systems, regenerative techniques, and best practices are all covered in detail in workshops, training sessions, and online resources. The impact of educational activities is further enhanced through collaborations among academic institutions, environmental organizations, and agricultural extension services. Through disseminating knowledge and promoting a comprehensive understanding of sustainable animal care, these initiatives aid in the widespread adoption of practices that put the well-being of communities, ecosystems, and animals at the forefront.

CHAPTER VI

Harvesting and Preserving

Efficient Harvesting Techniques

The final phase of the agricultural cycle, harvesting, is crucial in determining whether a farming project succeeds. In addition to increasing output, effective harvesting methods are essential for maintaining crop quality, minimizing post-harvest losses, and maximizing resource use. This section examines the various aspects of effective harvesting methods, including timing, equipment, technology, and environmentally friendly methods. Farmers can improve yield, lessen their environmental impact, and support the long-term sustainability of agricultural systems by adopting efficient harvesting practices.

A key component of effective harvesting is timing, which affects crop quality and yield. The right timing to harvest requires balancing several variables, including crop maturity, weather, and market demand. While postponing harvesting might result in overripe fruit, compromising quality and shelf life, it can lead to undeveloped crops with lesser yields. Keeping an eye out for signs of physiological maturity in crops, like color changes in fruits or grain drying out, can help determine the best time to harvest them. Harvesting decisions are also influenced by weather circumstances, such as approaching rain or unfavorable weather events. By utilizing contemporary technology like predictive modeling and remote sensing, farmers can maximize production and quality by harvesting at the ideal moment and making well-informed decisions based on real-time data.

Harvesting methods have undergone a revolution thanks to mechanization, which has improved productivity, speed, and labor savings. Harvesting is streamlined by equipment like combine harvesters, specialist fruit pickers, and automated systems, which decreases the need for manual labor and speeds up the harvesting process. For example, combine harvesters combine cutting, threshing, and winnowing tasks into one pass, significantly reducing the time and effort needed to harvest grains. Fruit-picking machines can collect ripe fruits selectively while causing the most minor damage to the crop, thanks to their robotic arms and sophisticated sensors. Mechanized harvesting improves accuracy, consistency, and overall efficiency in crop gathering while simultaneously addressing the labor crisis.

A new era of precision agriculture has begun thanks to technological advancements, where automation and data-driven insights maximize harvesting techniques. With sensors and monitoring equipment, Global Positioning System (GPS) technology makes it possible to map fields and apply variable-rate harvesting precisely. This helps farmers maximize resource utilization and reduce waste by customizing harvesting processes based on the unique features of various sections within a field. Uncrewed aerial vehicles (UAVs) or drones fitted with imaging sensors make real-time aerial views of crops possible. These views facilitate the evaluation of crop health, maturity, and uniformity. With the aid of these technology instruments, farmers may increase the sustainability and efficiency of their operations by using focused harvesting strategies and making well-informed decisions.

The long-term health of agricultural ecosystems and environmental care are given priority in sustainable harvesting practices. Reducing soil disturbance during harvest operations to stop erosion and maintain soil structure is one facet of sustainable harvesting. By improving water retention, encouraging beneficial microbial activity, and lowering soil erosion, conservation tillage or no-till farming practices contribute to soil health.

The remaining crop after harvest acts as organic mulch, which helps preserve soil even more. Sustainable harvesting also involves using water resources responsibly, particularly in areas where water is scarce. Using water-efficient harvesting methods and precision irrigation techniques can reduce water usage and lessen the environmental effect of agricultural operations.

Maximizing the advantages of harvesting requires effective post-harvest management. Harvested crops should be handled, stored, and transported correctly to avoid post-harvest losses and preserve product quality. Perishable products, like fruits and vegetables, benefit from rapid chilling or refrigeration because they prolong shelf life by slowing down physiological processes. Sufficient storage spaces, be they conventional barns, silos, or contemporary climate-controlled warehouses, are essential for maintaining the nutritional worth and commercial viability of harvested crops. Produce travels in the best condition when effective mechanisms, such as refrigerated trucks or containers, transport it. Adopting innovations such as modified environment packaging or controlled atmosphere storage extends the post-harvest life of crops, minimizes waste, and promotes sustainable food supply chains.

Efficient harvesting methods nevertheless need the human element, particularly for crops harvested by hand. The careful handling of crops, the deliberate selection of ripe fruit, and the general success of harvesting depend heavily on skilled labor. The workforce is more proficient when training programs emphasize quality control, ergonomics, and appropriate harvesting methods. Fair labor standards promote a happy workplace and aid in the retention of skilled workers. These policies include reasonable working hours and adequate salary. Community engagement and collaboration among agricultural communities create a supporting ecosystem for sustainable agriculture, which further improves the collective knowledge and effectiveness of harvesting procedures.

Enhancing biodiversity and resilience in agricultural systems, crop variety, and integrating agroecological principles contribute to effective harvesting procedures. More diverse cropping methods, such as polyculture or intercropping, spread out the risk of crop failure and lessen crop vulnerability to pests and diseases. Moreover, varied plants encourage natural predators and reduce the need for chemical inputs by building a more resilient and complex ecosystem. Agroecological practices improve soil health, nutrient cycling, and overall ecosystem balance. Examples of these practices include the use of cover crops, crop rotations, and beneficial insect habitats. Farmers that adopt these techniques improve harvesting efficiency and promote regenerative and sustainable agricultural systems.

The kind of crop and the particular circumstances of each farming operation influence the adoption of different harvesting procedures. For example, due to limited resources and lack of access to machinery, small-scale or subsistence farmers may still use traditional methods, such as manual harvesting and processing. Large-scale commercial activities, however, frequently make use of Cutting-edge technologies and automated processes to maximize productivity. Regardless of size, a comprehensive strategy for effective harvesting considers agricultural production's social, economic, and environmental facets to strike a balance that will guarantee the farming practices' long-term sustainability.

In summary, effective harvesting methods are critical to agricultural projects' prosperity and long-term viability. Harvesting operations are optimized when timing, mechanization, technology, sustainable practices, post-harvest management, human aspects, and agroecological concepts are carefully considered. The future of practical and ethical harvesting will be significantly influenced by incorporating cutting-edge technologies, sustainable practices, and community involvement as agriculture develops. Farmers who use an efficient harvesting strategy optimize the returns on their work and advance the more general objectives of food security, environmental conservation, and sustainable resource utilization.

Canning and Preserving Your Bounty

It is a long-standing custom to preserve the harvest's abundance so that people can enjoy the taste of fresh produce all year long. Fruits, vegetables, and other perishables have a longer shelf life when canned and preserved, and they also maintain the essence of seasonal bounty. This section explores the different techniques, tools, and factors involved in this culinary activity as it dives into the art and science of canning and preserving. A road toward self-sufficiency, decreasing food waste, and savoring the flavor of deliciously preserved food can be taken by anybody, from traditional water bath canning to contemporary pressure canning and alternative preservation methods.

Water bath canning is one of the most accessible and popular types of home canning. This technique works well with foods with high acid content, like fruits, pickles, jams, and items made from tomatoes, since the acidity makes it difficult for dangerous germs like Clostridium botulinum to grow. Jars containing ready-to-eat food are immersed in boiling water for a certain amount of time during the water bath canning process. As the jars cool, the vacuum seal created by the heat prevents the entry of additional contaminants by killing bacteria and mold. Because it requires little specialist equipment and offers a simple procedure for preserving fruits and vegetables at their optimal freshness, water bath canning is an excellent place for beginners to start.

Pressure canning is the suggested technique for low-acid foods to guarantee safety and lower the danger of botulism. Soups, meats, poultry, and vegetables are examples of low-acid foods. A specialized pressure canner can raise temperatures above those attained during water bath canning, which is how pressure canning works. To guarantee the safety of the preserved food, the high temperature is essential for eliminating the Clostridium botulinum spores. A pressure gauge is included with pressure canners to help regulate and monitor internal pressure, creating an atmosphere ideal for destroying dangerous germs. Although pressure canning might appear more involved than water bath canning, it offers a dependable and adaptable method for preserving various foods with longer shelf life.

Different preserving methods provide ways to conserve and savor seasonal harvests besides canning. One easy way to keep fruits, vegetables, and even herbs fresh is to freeze them. It's quick and easy. To preserve texture and flavor, the produce is immediately frozen after a brief blanching to stop enzymatic activity. Not everything freezes well, but berries, peas, maize, and other foods that thaw well are good candidates for freezing. Drying, or dehydration, is another age-old technique for food preservation. Dehydration stops spoiling by taking away moisture, which prevents bacteria from growing. Due to their low weight, dehydrated fruits, vegetables, and herbs are convenient to store and can be used in various culinary applications.

Foods can be preserved through fermentation, which improves the meal's nutritional value and flavor while extending its shelf life. Microorganisms like bacteria and yeast break down food's sugars and starches during fermentation, producing lactic acid or alcohol. This food is preserved and given distinctive flavors because the acidic environment inhibits the growth of dangerous bacteria. Pickles, yogurt, kimchi, and sauerkraut are examples of common fermented foods. Enabling natural microbial activity to convert raw foods into tart, probiotic-rich treats is the fermentation process. In addition to preserving the bounty, fermentation enhances the culinary experience by giving regular meals new flavors and textures.

The skill of canning and preserving gains a new depth by preserving herbs and aromatic plants. Herb-infused oils and vinegar provide a delicious pop to food and are simple to make at home. Fresh herbs such as basil, thyme, or rosemary can be steeped in oils or vinegar to make unique concoctions that improve the flavor of cooked foods, marinades, and salads. The infusions can be preserved in sterile bottles and used to infuse food items with a hint of herbal flavor. Herbs can also be dehydrated or air-dried to make homemade spice blends, guaranteeing a year-round supply of flavorful flavors.

Fruit selection of the highest caliber is essential to effective canning and preservation. Selecting produce at the height of its ripeness guarantees that the preserved final product retains its maximum nutritional value and flavor. Making that either overripe or underripe might make inferior preserves with weak flavors and a weakened texture. Choose fresh, premium vegetables for canning and preservation projects from farmers' markets, pick-your-own farms, or home gardens. Participating in these activities also helps people develop a relationship with the seasons and an appreciation for each season's various flavors and natural cycles.

Successful canning and preservation depend critically on good sanitation and cleanliness. Thorough cleaning and sanitization of jars, lids, and utensils is necessary to remove any contaminants that can jeopardize the safety and quality of the preserved food. Sterilizing jars before adding prepared components is one of the most critical steps in establishing an environment conducive to preservation. Produce handling requires careful attention to hygiene as well. To avoid introducing hazardous bacteria, surfaces should be maintained clean, and hands should be thoroughly cleaned. For home-canned goods to be safe, processing periods and procedures must be followed precisely for each type of food. Following the proper protocols reduces the possibility of contracting foodborne illnesses and promotes the production of preserves of the highest caliber.

In addition to providing a helpful way to handle seasonal surpluses, canning and preserving support sustainable lifestyle choices. People can adopt a more self-sufficient and environmentally friendly lifestyle by reducing food waste and decreasing their dependency on commercially processed meals. More control over the ingredients can be achieved at home canning, allowing people to avoid preservatives, chemicals, and excess salt or sugar frequently present in store-bought canned items. Canning and preserving give people a creative outlet and a stronger bond with their food by letting them experiment with flavors, combinations, and methods.

Community involvement and knowledge exchange are essential in the realm of canning and preserving. A rich tapestry of shared experiences and insights is created through internet forums, community workshops, and traditional recipes passed down through the centuries. Working together creates possibilities to learn from the collective experience of those who have mastered the art of preservation and strengthens bonds between participants. From jam-making classes to pickling parties, these group activities not only build community ties and offer valuable skills but also transform the canning and preserving process into a communal celebration of food, culture, and sustainability.

Creating a Homestead Pantry

A growing number of people are turning to the establishment of homestead pantries to achieve self-sufficiency and a more environmentally friendly lifestyle. An idea of a farmhouse pantry that goes beyond the traditional concept of storing non-perishable goods reflects a dedication to resiliency, resourcefulness, and a connection to the land. This section investigates the idea of establishing a homestead pantry, looking into its significance, the components necessary for its creation, and the advantages it provides for different groups and individuals.

A homestead pantry is, at its core, a method of food storage that is strategic and planned, and it is aligned with the ideas of homesteading, which is a way of life that emphasizes self-sufficiency, simplicity, and a harmonious relationship with the environment. A homestead pantry expands the concept of a traditional pantry, which allows for storing extra goods. However, a homestead pantry encompasses a broader range of sustainable living practices. Not only does it become a hub for the preservation of food, but it also becomes a hub for cultivating a robust and diverse ecosystem within one's private residence.

The ability to store the bounty that comes with changing seasons is the cornerstone of a homestead pantry. The art of food preservation is an essential skill for homesteaders, and it includes everything from fermenting pickles and preparing jams to canning your fruits and vegetables. Using this method not only assures a continuous supply of flavorful and healthy food throughout the year but also reduces the amount of reliance on products that have been processed commercially. In its most basic form, a well-stocked farmhouse pantry is a demonstration of the capacity to make use of the abundant resources that nature provides and to store them for later use.

A wide variety of items can be found in a farmhouse pantry. These include fermented foods, dried herbs, fermented foods, staple grains, and legumes. Rice, wheat, and oats are grains that serve as the backbone of the food chain, offering both sustenance and variety. Beans and lentils are examples of legumes that contribute to a protein-rich diet. The pantry is not restricted to the essentials; rather, it encompasses a wide range of preserves, ranging from tomato sauce created at home to fruit preserves and sauerkraut that have been aged. In the same way, homesteaders strive to promote biodiversity in their gardens and on their land; the variety of things found in the pantry will reflect that diversity.

In addition, a farmhouse pantry is not only about food; rather, it encompasses a more comprehensive idea of sustainability. In addition to imparting taste to food, herbs, and spices cultivated at home also have therapeutic benefits, promoting a holistic approach to health and wellness. Probiotics, beneficial to the gut's health, are introduced into the diet by consuming fermented foods like kimchi and kombucha. As a result, the pantry of the farmhouse becomes a repository of both sustenance and well-being, exemplifying the interdependence of nutrition and health.

An individual embarks on a skill development journey when they begin developing and maintaining a homestead pantry. Techniques such as canning, fermenting, and dehydrating are examples of time-honored practices that have been handed down from generation to generation. Homesteaders not only show respect for techniques that have been around for centuries, but they also equip themselves with the knowledge necessary to break free from the cycles of consumerism by adopting these methods. Food preservation is a kind of self-sufficiency that communities may pass down to develop collective resilience. It is a skill that can be shared among members of the community.

Beyond the benefits to one's well-being, the benefits of establishing a homestead pantry are extensive. In a world characterized by unpredictability, such as the effects of climate change and changes in the economy, a homestead pantry serves as a buffer against the impact of external shocks. It provides a level of food security that is not dependent on the uncertainties associated with the market fluctuations. People and communities can protect themselves from the vulnerabilities exposed during crises by decreasing their reliance on commercial supply networks.

Additionally, a homestead pantry contributes to the preservation of the natural environment. By putting more of an emphasis on homegrown produce and preservation methods, the carbon footprint that is connected with transportation and industrial food processing can be reduced. The use of homestead pantries, examples of localized food systems, helps to alleviate the demand placed on natural resources and increase biodiversity by providing support for a wide range of crops and heritage varieties. Not only does a homestead pantry have a minor impact on the environment, but it also corresponds with regenerative farming practices, which help to promote a healthier relationship between humans and the world.

Additionally, establishing a homestead pantry fosters community among its members. Individuals who share the same aim can form bonds with one another through the exchange of information regarding food preservation, gardening, and sustainable living practices. During times of crisis, a community of homesteaders might assist by exchanging surplus commodities, expertise, and guidance with one another. This community component helps to reinforce the fabric of local communities, which fosters resilience in the face of challenges from the outside world.

A homestead pantry is not simply about stockpiling food;

it is a commitment to a way of life that values self-sufficiency, sustainability, and community. In conclusion, creating a homestead pantry is about more than just storage. The pantry becomes a living testament when it comes to the skills, knowledge, and values handed down from generation to generation. It represents the ability of individuals and groups to adapt to new circumstances and prosper in a constantly evolving world. By establishing a homestead pantry, one not only ensures that they have access to a source of sustenance but also contributes to a more sustainable and interrelated way of life.

CHAPTER VII

Water and Energy Independence

Implementing Rainwater Harvesting

Sustainable approaches to water management are desperately needed as the world's population continues to grow, and the effects of climate change worsen the problems associated with water scarcity. An increasingly popular approach is rainwater harvesting, an age-old method revitalized by contemporary technology and ecological consciousness. The importance of installing rainwater harvesting systems is examined in this section, along with its guiding principles, techniques, and the numerous advantages it provides for people, communities, and the environment.

Rainwater harvesting is a tried-and-true method of collecting and storing rainwater for multiple applications. Its foundation is the knowledge that rain, a plentiful and accessible resource, may be used to meet water needs for industry, agriculture, and homes. Rainwater harvesting is gathering rainwater from surfaces, such as rooftops, and storing it in underground reservoirs or tanks. After being obtained, this water can be utilized for flushing toilets, irrigation, and, with the proper preparation, even as a potable water source.

Optimizing the collection of precipitation runoff is a fundamental tenet of rainwater harvesting. Gutters and downspouts on roofs are part of roof catchment systems, which effectively direct rainfall into storage bins. This approach is suitable for both urban and rural environments because of its simplicity, which makes it simple to integrate into current structures. Furthermore, porous surfaces surrounding buildings, such as gravel or permeable pavers, improve groundwater recharge and inhibit soil erosion and surface runoff.

Rainfall-gathering techniques can be broadly divided into rooftop rainfall harvesting and surface runoff collection. Rainwater is gathered from open spaces, roadways, and other surfaces and sent to storage facilities through surface runoff harvesting. This technique, which focuses on capturing runoff during rain events, is instrumental in areas with intermittent but abundant rainfall. On the other hand, rooftop rainwater harvesting is increasingly prevalent in cities. Rainwater is gathered from rooftops and transported to storage tanks via gutters. This effective strategy works well in spaces where using open surfaces is restricted.

Rainwater collection has several advantages that touch on life's social, economic, and environmental aspects. Rainwater harvesting promotes sustainable water use by lessening the burden on conventional water sources like rivers and groundwater. Rainwater collection reduces the likelihood of flooding and soil erosion, promoting conservation and better water quality in nearby water bodies.

Additionally, rainwater gathering lessens reliance on centralized water supply networks, particularly in cities. The diversification of water sources improves resilience against disruptions caused by climate change or infrastructural breakdowns. Rainwater harvesting systems help communities become more self-sufficient by preparing them to deal with water shortages and interruptions in the municipal water supply.

Rainwater collection has the potential to save money for both individuals and communities. The long-term savings on water bills and possible savings on infrastructure maintenance for centralized water supply systems outweigh the initial cost of putting up a rainwater gathering system. Rainwater collection is a valuable technique for small-scale farmers in agriculture because it offers a dependable and affordable water source for irrigation, boosting crop productivity and revenue.

One of rainwater harvesting's most significant social effects is its influence. A fundamental human right is the ability to access water, and rainwater harvesting democratizes this access by giving communities and individuals authority over their water supplies. Rainwater collecting can ease the burden on marginalized groups in areas where water shortage is an urgent problem by guaranteeing a steady and dependable water source for daily requirements.

Rainwater harvesting also promotes a feeling of empowerment and communal involvement. Planning, building, and maintaining rainwater harvesting systems can improve social ties and establish shared accountability for water management. Rainwater harvesting education programs can also equip people with the knowledge they need to maximize water use and support the sustainable growth of their local communities.

There are geographical restrictions on the use of rainwater harvesting. It is an adaptable system that can fit many land uses and climates. Rainwater gathering becomes essential for agricultural practices and human use in arid and semi-arid regions where water scarcity is a persistent problem. Installing rainwater harvesting systems can relieve pressure on the water infrastructure that is currently in place in urban areas that are seeing a high population increase and offer a sustainable solution to satisfy the increasing demand.

It is critical to recognize that various technological, governmental, and social elements interact to determine the effectiveness of rainwater collection projects. By encouraging policies, providing incentives, and establishing regulatory frameworks, governments and municipalities may significantly contribute to the growth of rainwater harvesting. Widespread adoption can be aided by financial incentives like tax rebates or subsidies for constructing rainwater collection equipment. Rainwater harvesting can also be guaranteed to be included in new construction and renovations by incorporating it into building rules and urban planning regulations.

Rainwater harvesting systems are made more effective by technological improvements. Advancements improve the quality of gathered rainwater in storage tank design, filtration systems, and water treatment technologies, which qualify it for a broader range of uses, including drinkable water production. The effectiveness of these systems is further enhanced by intelligent technologies that maximize rainwater collecting and distribution based on meteorological trends.

In conclusion, putting rainwater collection into practice is a practical and sustainable way to deal with the problems caused by water scarcity. Its many advantages include social empowerment, financial savings, and environmental preservation. By utilizing the abundant natural resources provided by rain, people and communities can lessen their dependency on non-renewable water sources, promote ecological equilibrium, and strengthen their ability to withstand the unpredictable effects of climate change. The adoption of rainwater collection is evidence of our capacity to adapt and flourish in balance with the environment, particularly in light of the impending increase in water scarcity.

Solar Power for the Homestead

Using solar energy on homesteads has become a game-changing technique in a time when sustainability and environmental awareness are prevalent. Solar power, generated by using the sun's energy, is a clean, renewable energy source that aligns with homesteading's core values of environmental stewardship and self-sufficiency. This section examines the importance of solar power adoption for the homestead, exploring its fundamental ideas, valuable uses, and the many advantages it offers to people, communities, and the environment.

The basic principle of solar power for the homestead is using solar photovoltaic (PV) panels to absorb sunlight and transform it into valuable electricity. When exposed to sunlight, the semiconductor materials in these panels — which are usually mounted on rooftops or other open spaces—produce direct current (DC) electricity. After that, inverters change the DC electricity into alternating current (AC), suitable for the electrical grid and standard home equipment. Solar power systems are a good fit for homesteads because of their scalability and decentralized nature, sometimes requiring them to be off the grid.

Solar power's guiding principles, which strongly emphasize sustainability, independence, and a good working relationship with the environment, fit in perfectly with the homesteading lifestyle. Homesteads can reduce their reliance on non-renewable resources like fossil fuels and reduce their carbon impact by harnessing the sun's energy. Homesteads are empowered to become energy producers rather than just consumers because of solar power's decentralized nature, which also helps them become resilient and self-sufficient in the face of energy uncertainty.

There are many valuable uses for solar energy on a homestead, including essentials and contemporary comforts. Solar energy can power water pumps, appliances, heating and cooling systems, lighting systems, and more, offering a dependable and sustainable energy source for everyday requirements. Thanks to developments in energy storage technologies, homesteads can now store excess solar energy in batteries to keep their lights on during overcast days or at night. This capacity is vital for off-grid homesteads, where solar power becomes a lifeline for maintaining basic operations.

Since solar power systems are a flexible option that can be adjusted to various climates and terrains, their installation on a homestead is not restricted by geography. Solar power provides an off-grid electrification option in isolated rural locations with limited access to centralized electrical systems. Solar panels can be built into existing buildings in urban and suburban environments, which helps to decentralize electricity generation and lessens the demand on centralized power plants. Solar energy is scalable and inclusive for homesteads of various shapes and sizes due to its versatility.

Using solar energy on the homestead has several advantages that span social, economic, and environmental spheres. Regarding the environment, solar energy considerably lowers the greenhouse gas emissions that come with using conventional energy sources. Air quality and climate change mitigation benefits solar power's emission-free electricity generation. Less reliance on fossil fuels reduces the environmental impact of transportation and resource exploitation, consistent with homesteading's sustainable living ideals.

From an economic standpoint, solar energy for the homestead results in lower long-term expenses. The installation of solar panels and associated equipment may seem like a significant initial expenditure, but over time, lower energy costs and, in certain situations, tax credits or government incentives make up for the cost. Solar-powered homesteads are immune to energy price fluctuations and offer stability in unpredictable economic times. In addition, homesteads can receive credits or payment from energy providers by feeding excess energy generated by the solar panels back into the grid.

Adopting solar power has equally critical social effects. Homesteads support community and individual energy security as they develop into self-sufficient energy producers. Because energy generation is becoming more decentralized, homesteads are more resilient. They can continue to provide essential services even during a power outage or other disturbance to the centralized grid. Solar power may close the energy gap in rural areas, where dependable access to electricity is sometimes problematic. This would empower local populations and enhance their quality of life in general.

Installing solar electricity also encourages a culture of environmental consciousness and responsibility. Solar-powered homesteads are role models for sustainable living, encouraging nearby populations to explore renewable energy options. Initiatives to educate people about solar power can teach them to use energy more efficiently and promote a deeper awareness of the interdependence of human activity and the environment.

Developments in solar technology enhance the efficiency and accessibility of solar power systems. Advancements improve the efficacy and dependability of solar power for the homestead in innovative grid technologies, energy storage options, and solar panel design. Homesteaders may grow their solar power capacity as needed thanks to modular and adaptable designs, which help them adjust to changing energy demands over time. Furthermore, as solar energy research and development continue to bring down costs, solar power is becoming more and more accessible and cheap for a more extensive range of homesteaders.

Governments and legislators also greatly aid in promoting the use of solar electricity. The switch to renewable energy sources, including solar electricity, can be accelerated with incentive programs, subsidies, and favorable legislation. The ability for homesteads to sell excess energy back to the grid through net metering incentivizes the use of solar power. Furthermore, mainstreaming solar power is aided by building rules and laws that either demand or encourage the integration of solar panels in new buildings.

Though solar power has many benefits for the homestead, there are drawbacks and things to consider. The variable patterns of sunlight present a constraint, necessitating the implementation of efficient energy storage strategies to guarantee an uninterrupted power supply. While lithium-ion batteries and other energy storage technologies are advancing, further progress in this field is still required to maximize the dependability of solar power systems. Furthermore, some homesteaders may find the upfront expense of installing solar panels to be a barrier, requiring them to make financial plans and seek out financing solutions.

The homestead's decision to switch to solar power signifies a paradigm leap toward a more robust and sustainable way of life. It embodies the values of environmental conservation, self-sufficiency, and a dedication to lessening our ecological imprint. Solar energy integration into homesteads is positioned to become more than simply a fad. Instead, it will become a fundamental component of a more sustainable and regenerative future as solar technology develops and the world's attention toward sustainability grows. Homesteaders set a path toward energy independence, environmental responsibility, and peaceful coexistence with the natural world by harnessing the sun's power.

Reducing Your Environmental Footprint

People worldwide are realizing how important it is to reduce their ecological footprint in the face of growing environmental difficulties. Reducing one's environmental footprint is now a fundamental component of sustainable living, which recognizes that human decisions, actions, and consumption patterns all impact the environment's state. This section explores the importance of lessening your environmental impact by reviewing the fundamental ideas, doable tactics, and broader ramifications of leading a more sustainable lifestyle.

Fundamentally, the environmental footprint is the sum of a person's or a community's actions on the environment. It includes many elements, such as trash production, resource consumption, carbon emissions, and general ecological deterioration. Understanding this effect causes people to perceive things differently, accepting accountability for their part in the environment's decline and making a concerted effort to leave as little of a trace as possible.

It takes a diverse strategy to reduce one's environmental footprint, considering different facets of daily living. The primary tenet is to promote resource efficiency—maximizing the utility obtained from available resources while reducing waste. This idea applies to every element of life, including eating preferences, purchasing behavior, and transportation and energy use decisions. People can reduce their environmental effects significantly by adopting a resourcefulness and mindful decision-making mindset.

Because energy consumption is directly related to carbon emissions and climate change, it is a critical component of the environmental footprint. A big step in lowering the carbon footprint connected with energy use is switching to renewable energy sources, such as solar or wind power. Furthermore, a more sustainable energy profile can be achieved by taking easy steps like shutting off lights, utilizing energy-efficient appliances, and insulating homes. Making thoughtful transportation decisions, like taking the bus, carpooling, or buying an electric car, helps reduce the carbon emissions of individual travel.

Our dietary choices have a significant influence on how we affect the environment as well. Reduce the ecological footprint of food production by switching to a plant-based diet or increasing the amount of plant-based meals in your diet. One way to lessen the impact of livestock agriculture, a significant cause of deforestation and greenhouse gas emissions, is to adopt a more plant-based and sustainable diet. In addition to reducing food's carbon footprint through reduced transportation and environmentally friendly farming methods, supporting local and organic agriculture also helps the environment.

Reducing waste is essential to lessening the influence on the environment. This entails using appropriate garbage disposal techniques and reducing the amount of waste produced. Choosing products with less packing, recycling, and composting are good ways to reduce waste's adverse environmental effects. The reduction of waste and the extraction of new resources are goals that align with the idea of a circular economy, in which things are recycled and repurposed instead of being thrown away.

In the perspective of trash reduction, the importance of lowering the usage of single-use plastics cannot be emphasized. Because of their environmental persistence and detrimental impacts on wildlife, plastics represent the more significant problem of disposable society. Reusable alternatives reduce the environmental impact of single-use plastics considerably. Examples include cloth bags, stainless steel water bottles, and containers. People may help reduce plastic pollution and promote responsible consumerism by encouraging a culture of reuse.

Another essential component of minimizing environmental effects is water conservation. The lack of freshwater supplies in many areas highlights the necessity for careful water use. Common sense measures like leak repair, water-efficient appliance use, and rainwater collection systems aid sustainable water management. Individual contributions to water conservation are further enhanced by conscious attempts to limit water use in daily activities, such as taking shorter showers and shutting off faucets when not in use.

Reducing one's environmental impact involves more than just personal behavior; it also requires consumer decisions. Encouraging businesses and goods that use sustainable production techniques, ethical sourcing methods, and solid environmental commitments sends a strong message to industries. Consumers who purchase secondhand goods or products with eco-friendly certifications make decisions consistent with their ethical and ecological consumerism beliefs. Consumer behavior is changing, which might lead to systemic change by pushing companies to prioritize sustainability.

It is impossible to overstate the importance of awareness-raising and education to lessen environmental footprints. Making educated decisions and being aware of how various activities affect the environment are the first steps. Formal and informal education programs help spread the word about the connection between environmental health and human activity. Education catalyzes conscious living and well-informed decision-making, and it can take many forms, from internet resources and movies to schools and community events.

Reducing one's environmental footprint has ramifications for global sustainability and personal well-being—issues including pollution, deforestation, biodiversity loss, and climate change demand coordinated action. Even though individual actions might not seem much in isolation, millions of people making sustainable decisions over time can have a substantial positive impact. The trajectory of environmental degradation may change if sustainable agriculture, renewable energy, and ethical consumer behaviors are adopted globally.

Reducing environmental footprints also promotes a feeling of fulfillment on a personal level and a connection to the natural world. People actively participating in sustainable practices frequently report feeling more purposeful and well-being. Mental and emotional well-being is enhanced by engaging in eco-friendly activities, enjoying the outdoors, and appreciating nature. The inextricable link between pleasure and environmental stewardship highlights the mutually beneficial interaction between humans and the environment.

In summary, minimizing your environmental impact involves a fundamental mindset shift that acknowledges the significant influence of human actions on the environment, not just a lifestyle decision. Individuals can help the global sustainability movement by adopting sustainable habits in energy use, food choices, waste management, and consumer behavior. A dedication to resource efficiency, thoughtful decision-making, and a deep comprehension of the relationship between individual decisions and the state of the environment marks the path to a reduced environmental impact. People who take on the duty of ecological stewardship actively participate in the more significant effort to create a more resilient and sustainable future.

CHAPTER VIII

Homesteading in Urban and Suburban Spaces

Adapting Homesteading Practices to Limited Spaces

In reaction to urbanization and constrained living spaces, homesteading—traditionally linked with vast rural vistas and independent living—is changing. Even in small urban or suburban areas, the homesteading tenets of self-reliance, sustainable agriculture, and a connection to the land can be made to work. The art of modifying homesteading methods for constrained places is examined in this section, along with the difficulties, creative fixes, and diverse advantages that result from combining sustainable living with urban limitations.

Space constraints are the most obvious obstacle to integrating homesteading methods in urban settings. Homesteaders in urban areas are challenged to make the most of every square inch that may be used for farming. Vertical planting is an important option that turns walls and balconies into valuable areas. Homesteaders can maximize vertical space for agricultural reasons by growing herbs, vegetables, and even small fruit-bearing plants through hanging planters, vertical shelves, and container gardening.

In particular, container gardening is a flexible method for people with little area. Homesteaders can cultivate various crops on patios, rooftops, or even windowsills using pots, raised beds, and other containers. In addition to making the most of available space, container gardening allows plants to be relocated to receive the most solar exposure or shelter from inclement weather. This flexibility is particularly useful in urban settings where shared or restricted outdoor spaces may exist.

Microgreens and sprouting are other effective methods for incorporating fresh food into a homesteader's diet in a limited space. These fast-growing, highly nutrient-dense plants can be grown inside with little room and input. Microgreen trays fit neatly on a windowsill or countertop, offering a steady supply of fresh, organic greens all year round. This approach highlights the value of nutrient-rich, locally-grown vegetables in urban homesteading while simultaneously addressing space constraints.

A crucial element of modifying homesteading methods to fit in constrained areas is reconsidering the care of livestock and other animals. Larger animals like chickens, goats, or rabbits may be allowed on traditional homesteads, but urban homesteaders must consider other choices. For smaller places, micro-livestock like dwarf goats or quail can be regarded as. In addition, backyard poultry, particularly hens, are becoming increasingly popular in cities. Chickens are a good alternative for people looking to incorporate animal husbandry into constrained settings because of their small coops, meticulous waste control, and noise tolerance.

A key component of sustainable urban homesteading, composting solves trash management and space issues. Homesteaders can turn kitchen leftovers into nutrient-rich compost using small composting systems like worm bins or Bokashi composting. This provides a valuable resource for improving the soil in container gardens and tiny planting spaces and lowering the quantity of garbage dumped in landfills. Even in the middle of metropolitan settings, the closed-loop nature of composting is in perfect harmony with the ecological ideals of homesteading.

Innovative options for urban homesteaders wishing to grow food in a resource- and space-conscious way include hydroponics and aquaponics. These soilless growth techniques do not require standard soil beds since they feed plants with nutrient-rich water. By fusing hydroponic gardening with aquaculture, aquaponics creates a symbiotic system in which plant waste supplies nutrients to fish waste and filter fish water. Urban homesteaders will find this closed-loop system a very efficient option because it can be customized to meet a variety of indoor and outdoor areas.

Water management becomes an essential factor to consider while modifying homesteading methods for smaller areas. Effective irrigation systems are necessary in urban areas because of the frequent restrictions and lack of water. For urban homesteads, drip irrigation, soaker hoses, and rainwater collection are essential elements of sustainable water management. Rainwater can be collected using rain barrels or small-scale water catchment systems, which lessens the need for municipal water supply and the environmental effect of water use.

Increasing efficiency in constrained areas also involves integrating technology. Innovative gardening equipment, automation systems, and sensors enable urban homesteaders to monitor and manage their small farms precisely. Homesteaders can maximize growing conditions and maximize resource utilization with the help of automated irrigation, climate management, and lighting systems. Urban homesteaders embrace technology while striking a balance, using innovation to improve sustainability without sacrificing the core ideas of self-sufficiency.

An essential component of successful urban homesteading is community engagement. Collaborative projects, shared areas, and gardens can increase the effect of individual efforts. Urban homesteaders can pool resources, exchange expertise, and work together to solve problems through community gardens. Urban homesteaders can work together to overcome space constraints and create vibrant pockets of sustainable living inside the urban fabric by promoting a feeling of community.

Advocacy and education are also essential in helping to modify homesteading methods for constrained areas. By sharing their successes, expertise, and experiences with their neighbors, urban homesteaders can promote a more comprehensive understanding of sustainable living. Workshops, neighborhood get-togethers, and educational programs can encourage people to adopt homesteading techniques, which will spread sustainability throughout urban areas.

The advantages of modifying homesteading methods for constrained areas go well beyond private houses. Urban homesteading lessens the environmental effects of industrial agriculture and long-distance transportation by promoting localized food production. Small-scale farming of various crops enhances biodiversity and builds resilience against climatic shifts and ecological uncertainty. Furthermore, the emphasis on environmentally friendly methods like rainwater collection and composting helps maintain the general health of urban ecosystems.

Urban homesteading questions accepted ideas about the production and consumption of food from a societal standpoint. It forces a reassessment of the urban environment and promotes the inclusion of green areas and sustainable development techniques in urban planning. The growing number of people choosing to homestead in constrained areas creates a demand for organic, locally-grown produce, encouraging businesses and policymakers to promote sustainable agriculture efforts. Urban homesteading thus serves as a trigger for more extensive structural change.

To sum up, modifying homesteading techniques to fit constrained areas is an innovative way to deal with the difficulties of city living. Sustainable living is not limited to rural areas, as demonstrated by the tenacity and inventiveness of urban homesteaders. Even in the middle of concrete jungles, urban homesteaders are fostering a harmonious relationship with the soil through creative animal husbandry, vertical gardening, container farming, composting, and other practices. The lessons gained from modifying homesteading methods to constrained areas become more pertinent as the world's population continues to urbanize; they provide a roadmap for a more resilient, sustainable, and linked urban future.

Community Homesteading Initiatives

Community homesteading efforts are gaining traction in the quest for resilient communities and sustainable living. These programs, based on environmental stewardship, self-sufficiency, and teamwork, unite community members to manage and nurture common areas, engage in sustainable agriculture, and develop a stronger bond with the land. This section examines the importance of communal homesteading projects, going into their guiding ideals, real-world implementations, and significant effects on people and communities.

Initiatives centered around community homesteading are based on independence and mutual accountability principles. By combining their resources, abilities, and efforts, these programs encourage people in a community to come together and build a resilient and sustainable living environment. In contrast to conventional homesteading, typically connected to individual homes or families, community homesteading broadens the definition to encompass a group of people committed to sustainable practices and the community's welfare.

Cultivating shared spaces is one of the cornerstones of community homesteading projects. Green areas, orchards, and community gardens serve as gathering places where locals actively engage in growing fruits, vegetables, and herbs together. In addition to supporting regional food production, these shared areas help people feel more connected to one another as they work side by side and exchange insights, stories, and the products of their labor. Creating shared spaces emphasizes the idea that a community grows and thrives together, and doing so becomes a sign of communal resilience.

Sustainable farming methods are essential to the accomplishment of neighborhood homesteading projects. Composting, water conservation, and organic farming practices are advocated among the locals. Community homesteading projects prioritize biodiversity and soil health to establish healthy ecosystems in suburban or urban settings. This focus on sustainable agriculture reduces conventional agricultural practices' environmental impact while ensuring a local, fresh food supply.

In some communal homesteading programs, cultivating shared spaces goes beyond typical gardening, including animal husbandry and animals. Beekeeping, small-scale poultry raising, and even shared apiaries add to the community homesteading model's diversity and adaptability. Recognizing the interdependence of humans and animals, these programs help the community develop a more comprehensive view of sustainable living.

Permaculture concepts are frequently at the heart of neighborhood homesteading projects. Derived from "permanent agriculture" or "permanent culture," permaculture is a design philosophy aiming to build self-sufficient, sustainable systems reminiscent of natural ecosystems. Permaculture design and management principles are applied to communal homesteading to create shared places that are productive, ecologically harmonious, and regenerative. This strategy promotes long-term sustainability by encouraging communities to imitate the resilience and patterns observed in nature.

Initiatives for community homesteading go beyond cultivating common areas to include more expansive living options. Residents are encouraged to implement sustainable house practices, such as water conservation, trash reduction, and using energy-efficient equipment. A culture of environmental responsibility is promoted, and individual habits are influenced by the community's collective commitment to sustainable living. Community homesteading projects catalyze a more significant cultural shift toward sustainable living by adopting common ideals and practices.

Community homesteading projects are fundamentally based on education and skill exchange. Classes, workshops, and group learning activities are planned to provide locals with the information and abilities required for sustainable living. Subjects covered include food preservation and alternative energy technology to organic gardening and permaculture design. This focus on education encourages a sense of empowerment and communal resilience and provides people with the means to engage in the homesteading project actively.

When it comes to community homesteading, achieving food sovereignty becomes imperative. Community members take charge of their local food supply chain by developing and producing their food. This independence lessens reliance on other sources, guarantees access to wholesome, fresh products, and promotes a sense of food security among community members. A vital resource during external disruptions like supply chain problems or natural calamities is the community's capacity to feed itself locally cultivated food.

The neighborhood as a whole gains from community homesteading projects and individual households. As neighbors cooperate on projects, tend to communal gardens, and take turns cleaning common areas, social ties strengthen. A more robust social fabric is produced by shared accountability and joint ownership, strengthening ties between neighbors. Consequently, this social resilience is a valuable advantage during challenging times since close-knit groups may help one another out.

Another significant result of communal homesteading programs is economic resiliency. Community members support the local economy by lowering their dependency on outside sources for resources and food. Local markets, barter networks, and community-supported agriculture (CSA) programs foster stronger economic relationships within the community and encourage the development of a more resilient and sustainable economic model. The reduction of carbon emissions linked to long-distance freight transportation, the creation of jobs locally, and local entrepreneurship are all financial advantages of communal homesteading.

Community homesteading efforts have a substantial ecological impact. Communities actively support environmental conservation by emphasizing eco-friendly technologies, limiting trash, and implementing sustainable agriculture. Permaculture-inspired communal areas serve as refuges for various wildlife species, thereby bolstering the well-being of nearby ecosystems. Community homesteading activities are further aligned with larger environmental aims by decreasing the carbon footprint associated with food production and consumption.

Municipalities and governments are essential in encouraging and supporting neighborhood homesteading projects. The success of these efforts is attributed to policies that support the establishment of community gardens, offer incentives for sustainable practices, and ease access to shared resources. For urban agriculture and communal homesteading initiatives to be legally compliant and practically feasible, zoning laws supporting them are crucial. Governments play an essential role in fostering the growth of more socially cohesive, resilient, and sustainable neighborhoods by sponsoring community homesteading programs.

To sum up, communal homesteading programs offer a creative and dynamic way to live sustainably within the confines of an urban or suburban setting. Based on the values of independence, teamwork, and environmental protection, these programs build strong, resilient communities that actively participate in shared resource management, sustainable agriculture, and developing a closer bond with the land. Community homesteading projects serve as rays of light amidst the ominous global issues of climate change, resource depletion, and food shortages. They demonstrate the transforming power of group action in creating a more linked and sustainable future.

Overcoming Challenges in Urban Homesteading

The discipline of developing self-sufficiency and sustainable living in urban environments, or "urban homesteading," presents a unique set of difficulties that call for resourcefulness and resilient attitudes. In densely populated concrete jungles, where land is scarce, laws are strict, and life moves quickly, urban homesteaders traverse a challenging terrain to grow food, care for small livestock, and adopt sustainable lifestyles. This section examines urban homesteaders' difficulties and digs into the creative fixes, flexibility, and collective fortitude that characterize this endeavor.

Space limitation is one of the main obstacles to urban homesteading. Land is scarce in highly populated urban areas, challenging conventional homesteading methods. Nonetheless, urban homesteaders have demonstrated skill in making the most of every inch used for farming. Vertical gardening emerges as a crucial tactic, converting rooftops, balconies, and walls into valuable areas. Urban homesteaders effectively exploit vertical dimensions for agriculture through hanging planters, shelving systems, and creative container gardening techniques, proving that a lack of horizontal space does not exclude the possibility of productive cultivation.

Urban homesteading finds that container gardening is a flexible way around space limits. Homesteaders can cultivate crops on patios, balconies, and window sills by using pots, raised beds, and other containers. Because containers are portable, it is possible to strategically expose plants to the sun or shield them from inclement weather. Not only is container gardening a valuable solution to space constraints, but it also represents the adaptability and inventiveness of urban homesteading, transforming even the most minor urban areas into fruitful, green havens.

Zoning laws and restrictions may restrict the activities that urban homesteaders are permitted to conduct on their residential holdings. Land use limits, garden structure prohibitions, and livestock regulations are expected in metropolitan areas. It takes a sophisticated grasp of local laws, good engagement with local government representatives, and occasionally pushing for reforms that support urban homesteading activities to get beyond these legal obstacles. Urban homesteaders successfully negotiate the regulatory environment by creating coalitions with like-minded community members and having productive conversations to help design laws promoting sustainable living.

Another major obstacle to urban homesteading is water management. Water shortage is a common problem in urban areas, and water restrictions imposed by the government may make it difficult to raise animals or maintain gardens. Water efficiency demands innovative irrigation techniques, like soaker hoses and drip watering. Rainwater harvesting systems provide a sustainable way to lessen the effects of water scarcity by utilizing rooftops or other impervious surfaces. These technologies generally help conserve water resources in metropolitan areas and reduce dependency on municipal water supply.

Particular difficulties for urban homesteaders engaged in animal husbandry are noise pollution and spatial constraints. It may be possible to keep traditional animals like chickens, rabbits, or miniature goats in a constrained metropolitan area, but careful planning will be needed to manage their living conditions. Urban homesteaders frequently turn to micro-livestock, like quail, which may produce eggs and meat while requiring less area and noise. Urban homesteaders can ethically integrate small-scale animal husbandry into their activities, fostering a connection to food sources in the middle of the city by choosing suitable breeds and putting soundproofing measures in place.

Composting is one of the cornerstones of sustainable living, but space constraints and smell concerns make it difficult in urban settings. Adopting small-scale composting solutions, like worm bins or Bokashi composting, which effectively processes kitchen scraps without emitting unpleasant odors, is necessary to overcome these obstacles. One way to reduce trash and improve soil is through community composting efforts, in which locals oversee composting systems together. Homesteaders actively help to close the loop in the urban food cycle and reduce the amount of trash transported to landfills by tackling the difficulties associated with composting in urban environments.

An essential component of overcoming obstacles in urban homesteading is community engagement. Collaborative projects, shared areas, and gardens increase the effect of individual work. Urban homesteaders can pool resources, exchange expertise, and work together to solve problems through community gardens. Urban homesteaders can fight for legislative changes, negotiate legal complications, and cultivate a sustainable culture in their neighborhoods by actively participating in the community. Collaborative endeavors and shared duties establish a network of support that turns disconnected urban homesteads into interconnected centers of sustainable living.

Due to the shadows of nearby structures, significant buildings, and small streets, urban homesteading frequently faces limited sunlight. Plant growth depends on adequate sunlight; urban homesteaders often have to arrange their gardens to get the most solar exposure. Furthermore, using reflective surfaces to reroute sunlight to plants in shadowed places is beneficial. Examples of these surfaces are mirrors and light-colored surfaces. To ensure that their crops receive enough light for healthy development, urban homesteaders should also investigate other approaches to additional illumination, such as using grow lights or reflecting materials.

Urban homesteaders can overcome obstacles with the help of technology. Homesteaders can achieve precision monitoring and control over small farms through automation systems, intelligent gardening tools, and sensors. Automated irrigation, climate control, and lighting systems are made possible by optimizing growing conditions and offsetting the limits of natural sunshine. Urban homesteaders embrace technology while striking a balance, using innovation to improve sustainability without sacrificing the core values of independence and connection to the natural environment.

Educational activities are essential in enabling urban homesteaders to overcome obstacles and create resilient communities. Workshops, neighborhood gatherings, and instructional initiatives offer insightful information on environmentally friendly procedures, ethical dilemmas, and creative fixes. Urban homesteaders foster a culture of ongoing learning in their communities by sharing their knowledge and experiences. Education projects act as accelerators for overcoming obstacles and creating a community spirit of urban homesteading by spreading knowledge and encouraging a culture of inquiry and innovation.

To sum up, the capacity to overcome obstacles in urban homesteading is a tribute to the grit, flexibility, and inventiveness of those who want to live sustainably in the middle of busy cities. Urban homesteaders use creativity and tenacity to overcome a challenging environment, including noise issues, water scarcity, zoning limitations, and restricted space. Urban homesteaders create sustainable urban oases through community involvement, vertical farming, container gardening, and intelligent technology utilization. As they overcome obstacles, urban homesteaders contribute to the Broader trend toward a more resilient, sustainable, and integrated urban future.

CHAPTER IX

Building Community Connections

Collaborative Homesteading Projects

Collaborative homesteading initiatives signify a paradigm shift in sustainable living as people unite to foster resilience, self-sufficiency, and a deep bond with the land. The concepts of traditional homesteading are applied to entire communities within the framework of these projects, encouraging knowledge sharing, shared duties, and a group commitment to sustainable practices. The importance of cooperative homesteading initiatives is examined in this section, along with its guiding ideas, valuable applications, and transforming effects on both the people involved and the communities they benefit.

The philosophy of group effort and shared accountability is the foundation of cooperative homesteading initiatives. In contrast to individual homesteading activities, including houses functioning independently, collaborative projects inspire community members to unite to support sustainable living. These initiatives can take many shapes, such as communal gardens, cooperative farms, or shared areas where people gather to raise animals, generate food, and embrace sustainable lifestyles. Collaborative homesteading relies heavily on pooling resources, talents, and efforts; this framework allows the entire community to actively participate in developing a sustainable lifestyle.

Community gardens are excellent examples of cooperative homesteading endeavors. Residents gather together in these communal areas to grow fruits, vegetables, and herbs. In addition to aiding in food production locally, community gardens serve as centers for social interaction, skill development, and information sharing. People take turns doing tasks like watering, weeding, and harvesting to create a sense of group ownership and a bond with the food they grow.

Community gardens are hubs for fostering a sense of community beyond the physical harvest, as neighbors work together to complete everyday undertakings that benefit the individual and the group.

Collaborative homesteading can also take the form of cooperative farms, where locals manage more considerable agricultural holdings together. These initiatives frequently entail the joint ownership and management of a farm, enabling people to take part in every step of the food production process—from planting and harvesting to distribution. Cooperative farms provide a more direct link between farmers and consumers, strengthening communal food sovereignty. By cooperating, community members share the effort and take on the risks and benefits of agriculture as a group, strengthening the system's resilience and interdependence.

In cooperative homesteading endeavors, common areas are utilized for conventional farming and small-scale animal husbandry, composting, and rainwater collection. The residents manage Composting systems cooperatively and use kitchen scraps to create nutrient-rich compost that improves the soil in community gardens. Collecting and storing rainwater, rainwater harvesting projects lessen reliance on municipal water supply for irrigation. Small-scale animal husbandry, like raising hens or bees, becomes a communal endeavor that offers communities beneficial pollination services, fresh eggs, and honey.

Collaborative homesteading initiatives require education and the sharing of skills. Classes, workshops, and group learning activities are planned to provide locals with the information and abilities needed for sustainable living. Subjects covered include food preservation and alternative energy technology to organic gardening and permaculture design. Collaborative initiatives establish a culture of continual learning within the community by providing a forum for exchanging traditional and experienced knowledge. When people share their knowledge, collective intelligence develops, strengthening the community's resilience.

Collaborative homesteading initiatives are frequently guided by permaculture principles, which offer a comprehensive framework for sustainable land use and design. Derived from "permanent agriculture" or "permanent culture," permaculture aims to build self-sufficient, regenerative systems that mimic natural ecosystems. Permaculture design ideas inform shared space layouts in cooperative homesteading, ensuring that the areas are functional and harmonious with the environment. By including a variety of plant species, companion planting, and soil-building methods, the community's agricultural practices become more resilient and help to create a regenerative and balanced environment.

Collaborative homesteading initiatives strongly emphasize resource efficiency, with participants aiming to maximize the utility obtained from available resources while avoiding waste. These programs are ingrained with the reduce, reuse, and recycle philosophy. Residents frequently share tools, equipment, and resources to reduce overall consumption and do away with the necessity for private ownership. A closed-loop system where organic waste is converted into compost and improves the soil in community gardens is made possible by composting systems and waste reduction techniques. Collaborative homesteading initiatives show a dedication to environmental stewardship by grouping to adopt resource-efficient measures.

Collaborative homesteading initiatives use the community's resiliency to overcome obstacles. Zoning limits, regulatory barriers, and space constraints are all overcome collaboratively through solid advocacy, coordinated efforts, and excellent communication. Through collaborative projects, residents can resolve legal issues, raise concerns, and develop policies that encourage sustainable living. People come together to overcome problems and turn them into opportunities for growth and transformation, demonstrating the power of a united community.

Water management is a common concern in cooperative homesteading endeavors, especially in urban settings where water shortage is frequently a problem. Collectively built rainwater collecting systems collect and hold rainwater to irrigate standard agricultural fields and community gardens. Using efficient irrigation techniques, such as soaker hoses or drip watering, reduces water consumption. Communities actively participate in water conservation through cooperative efforts, which is consistent with the values of sustainability and conscientious resource management.

Collaborative homesteading projects that practice animal husbandry face unique obstacles due to noise pollution and space constraints in urban settings. By choosing suitable breeds as a group, using soundproofing techniques, and following ethical guidelines for animal care, communities can include small-scale animal keeping in their initiatives. Micro-livestock, like quail, emerges as a feasible alternative that offers communities a long-term supply of meat and eggs. Collaborative homesteading initiatives overcome the difficulties in managing urban cattle by assigning shared responsibility and committing to ethical animal treatment.

Collaborative homesteading initiatives have advantages for the entire community and individual households. As neighbors cooperate on projects, tend to communal gardens, and take turns cleaning common areas, social ties strengthen. A more robust social fabric is produced by shared accountability and joint ownership, strengthening ties between neighbors. Consequently, this social resilience is a valuable advantage during challenging times since close-knit groups may help one another out.

Another significant result of cooperative homesteading initiatives is economic resiliency. Community members support the local economy by lowering their dependency on outside sources for resources and food. Local markets, barter networks, and community-supported agriculture (CSA) programs foster stronger economic relationships within the community and encourage the development of a more resilient and sustainable economic model. Collaborative homesteading offers financial advantages such as local entrepreneurship, employment generation, and a lower carbon footprint than long-distance goods transportation.

Sharing Excess Produce and Goods

Sharing excess produce and goods becomes a significant method to address social and environmental concerns with the goal of sustainable living and resilient communities. Based on resourcefulness, giving, and community connection, sharing extra stuff fosters an abundant culture while reducing the harmful effects of waste and overconsumption. The importance of sharing extra food and goods is examined in this section, along with its practical applications, guiding principles, and significant effects on people, communities, and the environment.

Sharing extra products and produce embodies the principles of resource optimization and mindful consumerism. This practice signifies a fundamental conceptual shift in a world where waste and excessive consumerism are significant causes of environmental deterioration. Fundamentally, it encourages people to evaluate their requirements, cut back on wasteful spending, and redistribute extra resources to people who might use them. Sharing things, be it extra produce from a backyard garden, extra groceries, or unused household equipment, encourages people to take responsibility for how their decisions affect the environment and the larger community.

Community gardens, where people grow fruits, vegetables, and herbs together, are excellent models of sharing excess products. The surplus generated in these communal areas frequently surpasses the urgent requirements of the involved individuals or households. Sharing excess with neighbors, community centers, or food banks is possible. Community gardens help ensure local food security by sharing extra production, and they also encourage a sense of shared responsibility for ensuring everyone has access to wholesome, homegrown food.

Local food-sharing programs have become more popular for dispersing extra produce among neighbors. Online communities, neighborhood bulletin boards, or structured neighborhood exchanges can facilitate exchanges of excess fruits, veggies, and other homemade goods. Their programs establish physical or virtual venues where people can give away what they have in excess, and others can profit from their contributions. Sharing strengthens ties between neighbors and creates networks based on mutual assistance and reciprocity.

Programs for recovering food are essential to distributing extra produce to a broader audience. Food banks, restaurants, and grocery shops work together to repurpose excess edibles that might otherwise wind up in landfills. By giving extra food to those in need, these initiatives combat food poverty, lessen waste, and protect the environment. Food recovery initiatives that share excess produce with others align with sustainability ideals, as they encourage resource conservation and reduce the environmental impact of food waste.

"Community fridges" and "free stores" expand on sharing excess products beyond food. These neighborhood-based projects entail creating locations where people may drop off unwanted goods and pick up necessities. Free stores establish decentralized, autonomous sharing systems for non-perishable goods, clothing, and home products. These areas promote a sense of collective ownership and encourage community involvement by facilitating people to share what they no longer need and get access to necessities.

Sharing extra products and produce helps to achieve the more general objectives of environmental sustainability and waste reduction. In a world driven by consumerism, when excess consumption and disposal are commonplace, sharing emerges as a practical means of keeping goods out of landfills. Sharing lessens the need for new production, conserves resources, and lessens the environmental effect of production, transportation, and disposal by extending the lifecycle of goods and produce. Sharing extra stuff turns into activism against the disposable culture.

Not only is it necessary to share extra products to protect the environment, but it also helps to solve social inequality. By guaranteeing that those with less means still have access to needs, sharing helps close the gap in economic opportunities. Sharing gives people access to goods that could otherwise be monetarily unaffordable, such as furniture, clothing, or necessities for the home. This inclusivity strengthens the belief that everyone, regardless of financial situation, deserves access to the resources required for a decent living by fostering a sense of communal support and solidarity.

The sharing economy has broadened the scope of surplus commodities sharing thanks to the efforts of community-driven initiatives and digital platforms. Peer-to-peer platforms facilitate the lending, borrowing, and sharing of a vast array of goods, including toys, books, equipment, and tools. This cooperative consumption method minimizes the need for new products, optimizes resource use, and fosters communal involvement. The sharing economy's enabling platforms help people adopt more sustainable and collaborative lifestyles instead of ownership-centric ones.

Sharing extra things promotes a culture of empathy, reciprocity, and connection, as well as the advantages of resource conservation and social support. Sharing strengthens a sense of community, whether by accepting what is provided or offering more stuff to others. Recognizing interdependence among community members fosters the development of social relationships and trust. Communities built on a sense of shared duty and belonging are resilient and can overcome obstacles as a group.

Promoting the habit of sharing excess produce and goods is primarily achieved through educational programs. People can learn more about the effects of their purchasing decisions and be motivated to adopt more sustainable practices by attending workshops, participating in community events, and running awareness campaigns. Programs for education could center on issues including reducing food waste, practicing responsible consumption, and the effects of excessive consumption on the environment. Education projects enable people to actively engage in the sharing economy and improve the well-being of their communities by spreading knowledge and encouraging a culture of responsible consumption.

Sharing excess products within communities is supported and made more accessible by local governments and municipalities. The legal and practical viability of initiatives such as food recovery programs, community fridges, and free shop establishments are enhanced by policies that support them. Municipalities also sponsor educational initiatives that promote sustainable consumption habits and the advantages of sharing. Local governments help build more resilient, socially cohesive, and ecologically conscious communities by promoting and assisting the sharing culture.

In conclusion, sharing extra commodities and produce can have a profoundly positive impact on communities and individuals. This practice opposes the dominant culture of disposability and overconsumption because it is based on sustainability, community resilience, and responsible consumption. Sharing becomes a catalyst for good, whether through local food-sharing programs, community gardens, or the sharing economy made possible by Internet platforms. Sharing extra products and produce creates a culture of plenty, empathy, and connection that builds the foundation for a more socially linked, equitable, and sustainable future.

The Importance of Homesteading Communities

Homesteading communities play a unique and vital part in the fabric of sustainable living because they are founded on the values of self-sufficiency, community, and a strong bond with the land. In a time of resource depletion, environmental concerns, and increased awareness of the effects of contemporary living, homesteading communities stand out as resilient role models for building a more sustainable future. The significance of homesteading communities is examined in this section, which also looks at their practical applications, guiding principles, and revolutionary effects on people's lives, families, and society.

The spirit of self-reliance, where people band together to live in harmony with the land, grow their food, and embrace sustainable practices, is at the core of homesteading communities. Homesteading communities value more direct and hands-on interaction with the environment than traditional urban or suburban living does. This deliberate move away from depending on outside systems for supplies, food, and energy not only lessens the ecological footprint of community members but also dramatically increases their sense of independence and connectedness to the natural world.

A fundamental principle of homesteading communities is that sustainability informs choices from energy use to food production. Through regenerative land management, organic farming, and permaculture, these communities put the well-being of their ecosystems first. Residents work together to cultivate communal areas for gardening, orchards, and cattle, actively contributing to producing seasonal, organic, and locally sourced food. Homesteading communities support preserving biodiversity, the soil's health, and the ecosystem's well- being using sustainable agricultural practices.

Homesteading communities are known for their collaborative spirit, fostered by shared tasks and group initiatives that promote a sense of interconnectivity. Homesteading communities are cooperative communities where members work together to accomplish shared objectives, whether it is through resource management, building environmentally friendly infrastructure, or growing communal gardens. This collective mentality transcends the usefulness of homesteading and develops into a social structure that fortifies ties between neighbors. Mutual support and a sense of community are forged through shared experiences of caring for animals, working the land, and overcoming obstacles associated with sustainable living.

Education is a fundamental aspect of homesteading communities, where the sharing of knowledge and skills becomes an essential aspect of everyday existence. Workshops, skill-sharing sessions, and group education opportunities enable community members to participate actively in homesteading practices. Subjects covered include everything from conventional craftsmanship and renewable energy systems to organic farming methods and permaculture design. Through education, homesteading communities promote a culture of ongoing learning, adaptability, and creativity, giving people the practical skills required for a sustainable life.

Permaculture concepts heavily influence the architecture and culture of homesteading communities. Derived from "permanent agriculture" or "permanent culture," permaculture is an all-encompassing method for creating sustainable systems based on natural ecosystems. Permaculture concepts inform shared space layouts in the context of homesteading, highlighting the value of ecological harmony, diversity, and regenerative processes. This strategy ensures that homesteading communities contribute to the long-term resilience and health of the land they manage in addition to meeting their immediate needs.

One of the main goals of homesteading communities is self-sufficiency, which shows up in many facets of daily existence. By producing as much food, energy, and goods as possible, locals want to lessen their reliance on outside networks and supply lines. Homesteading communities become more resilient to external shocks by utilizing sustainable water management techniques and renewable energy sources like solar or wind power. In addition to offering a sense of security, this emphasis on self-sufficiency supports a more decentralized and sustainable way of life.

One of the critical characteristics of homesteading communities is their emphasis on resilience; they actively plan for and adjust to a range of problems, such as shifting environmental conditions, economic conditions, and possible disruptions to established institutions. Homesteading communities lay the groundwork for navigating uncertainty by producing a variety of foods, conserving water, and developing alternate energy sources. Resilience in these communities goes beyond pragmatic concerns to include mental and emotional health, as members gain self-efficacy and self-assurance in their capacity to overcome obstacles.

Communities that practice homesteading are essential in promoting a waste- and resource-conscious society. These communities proactively reduce their ecological footprint through initiatives like composting, recycling, and upcycling. Waste becomes a valuable resource, with organic matter converted into nutrient-rich compost and discarded things recycled for various purposes. In addition to being in line with ecological ideals, the dedication to waste reduction also acts as a prototype for more significant societal movements toward more sustainable and circular economies.

Homesteading communities have stronger links to one another than just their immediate neighborhood; they also have broader networks of like-minded people. A shared sense of values and behaviors creates a supportive community that transcends geographical boundaries. A sense of unity and interconnectedness within the more significant homesteading movement is fostered by homesteading groups' frequent participation in knowledge-sharing forums, internet platforms, and cooperative projects with neighboring communities. These networks, in turn, become valuable tools for education, problem-solving, and assistance to one another.

Economic resiliency is a natural byproduct of the sustainability and self-sufficiency that homesteading groups practice. Reducing reliance on outside sources for products, energy, and food allows locals to support the local economy. Local markets, barter networks, and community-supported agriculture (CSA) programs foster stronger economic relationships within the community and encourage the development of a more resilient and sustainable economic model. The reduction of carbon emissions linked to long-distance freight transportation, the development of jobs locally, and local entrepreneurship are all examples of the economic benefits.

Homesteading communities regularly participate in ecological restoration and land management initiatives, demonstrating their dedication to environmental conservation. Permaculture-inspired communal areas serve as refuges for various wildlife species, thereby bolstering the wellbeing of nearby ecosystems. To further the larger objectives of ecological sustainability, homesteading communities' residents frequently take part in forestry campaigns, soil regeneration projects, and water conservation campaigns. Homesteading communities learn to care for the land and protect the natural resources they depend on by implementing these practices.

Homesteading communities rely heavily on their governments' and municipalities' support and encouragement. These communities succeed because of policies that support sustainable land use, offer financial incentives for using renewable energy, and make shared resources more accessible. Ensuring homesteading activities' legal and practical viability requires zoning restrictions that support these operations. Governments help create more resilient, socially cohesive, and sustainable communities by actively promoting homesteading communities.

To sum up, homesteading communities are actual instances of resilient and sustainable existence. These communities offer guidance for developing a peaceful coexistence between people and the environment by upholding the values of self-sufficiency, cooperation, and a strong bond with the land. With the rise of global issues like resource depletion, climate change, and social vulnerability, homesteading communities are becoming more and more critical. In addition to offering a workable example of sustainable living, they inspire optimism for a time when people coexist peacefully with the environment as individuals and groups.

CONCLUSION

In the pages of "Homesteading Harmony: Transform Your Backyard into a Self-Sufficient Haven," readers embark on a journey toward a more sustainable and fulfilling way of life. This e-book is a valuable resource for anybody looking to strengthen their ties to the land, become more self-sufficient, and develop resilience in the face of contemporary difficulties because of its thoughtful examination of homesteading ideas and methods.

As this comprehensive guide illustrates, homesteading is not just about growing your food—it's about embracing a new mindset and lifestyle. "Homesteading Harmony" empowers readers to redefine their relationship with the environment, prioritize sustainability, and take control of their lives through engaging narratives, practical advice, and a wealth of knowledge.

Readers are encouraged to grow their food and create a haven that embodies the beauty of a harmonious life by transforming their backyard into a self-sufficient paradise. The e-book explores the many aspects of homesteading, including permaculture design, energy-efficient techniques, organic gardening, and community involvement. It underscores the advantages of collaboration, shared values, and creativity, fostering a sense of community among homesteaders.

Readers will find the inspiration to take immediate steps towards a more sustainable lifestyle as they delve into the content. "Homesteading Harmony" is more than just a guide; it's a call to action, urging readers to adopt sustainable principles, develop eco-friendly habits, and contribute to the broader movement towards resilient and self-sufficient communities.

To sum up, "Homesteading Harmony" serves as a guide for anyone looking to embark on a life-changing path toward a more peaceful and sustainable living. This e-book is a priceless tool for anybody preparing to start a farm and create a life that speaks to balance, resilience, and harmony because of its abundance of ideas, practical advice, and vision for a self-sufficient haven in every backyard.

Thank you for buying and reading/listening to our book. If you found this book useful/helpful please take a few minutes and leave a review on the platform where you purchased our book. Your feedback matters greatly to us.